QUESTIONS GOD ASKS

...AND WHAT THE ANSWERS REVEAL ABOUT US.

BRYAN DUNHAM

INDEPENDENCE PRESS

Library of Congress Control Number: 2025927079

ISBN: 979-8-9932245-0-3

Printed in the United States of America

DEDICATION

This book is dedicated to: Erwin McManus, Rob Bell, Matt Chandler, John Ortberg, and Dallas Willard.

If discipleship is a relationship by which one life is helping another walk with God, then I have been discipled by spiritual giants. While you did not know you were discipling me specifically, you have forever shaped how I view God, the world He created, my role in it, and my place in it. I could never thank you enough.

-BD

CONTENTS

PREFACE

One day, while reading Luke 18, I came across the familiar story of a blind man brought to Jesus. Though I had read this story many times, this time I was arrested by the question Jesus asked him: "What do you want me to do for you?" (Luke 18:41).

Seriously? I was surprised by what, on the surface, appears to be the extreme ignorance of Jesus. Even I, reading this account some two-thousand years later, could guess his answer: "Lord, I want to see."

Jesus heals the man and everyone praises God. End of scene.

But I couldn't get this scripture out of my head. Suddenly I was seeing it differently. It was like the "glitch" in the movie *The Matrix*. It was a splinter in my mind. *Why does Jesus ask this question?* He is God. If the man's obvious blindness wasn't reason enough, wouldn't Jesus, by virtue of his divinity, already know exactly what this man wants?

Falling back on my training as a police officer, as I often did, I knew that when attempting to understand a situation you begin with the facts and those facts will lead you to questions. The facts are: God is omniscient – all knowing. Jesus is God incarnate. Therefore He knows everything past, present, and future. He has the hairs on our heads numbered. The man in the story is blind. He cries out to Jesus as he hears that Jesus is passing by. Jesus stops and calls for the man to be brought to him. This is when Jesus asks him the question. Jesus already knows exactly what the man wants him to do, before He asks. Those are the facts.

Here are the questions: Since Jesus is not asking the question to obtain information, then it must be for some other reason – what could that reason be? Is there some need this man has other than blindness that Jesus is trying to bring to his attention? Did Jesus know this man needed to name his need aloud – to experience the humility of voicing dependence? Could it be that it has nothing to do with the blind man, but someone else in the crowd that needed to hear Jesus ask him this question?

I didn't know the answer to those questions and the more I considered them the more questions I had. I wondered how many other questions Jesus asks in the gospel of Luke. I started in Luke 1 and tracked them. That led to uncovering all the questions Jesus asks in the gospels. It wasn't long after that I went back to the very beginning, Genesis 1, and started on a quest to look at all the questions God asks in the entire Bible.

It was fascinating to analyze the questions that an all-knowing God asks. It is a simple yet profound truth that He is not asking because he needs the information... but *because we need the answers.*

This opened up a perspective on the Bible I had never seen before.

Typically when I uncover insights in the Bible, I make notes on it, pray about its application to my life, and then file it away on my laptop for potential future use in a sermon.

I started to do that with this subject, but the sheer volume of the questions, combined with significant insights had me saying to the low glow of my laptop early one weekday morning, "This... should be a book."

Now it is.

Writing this book has changed me. I hope that reading it changes you.

San Antonio, Texas

September 2025

Bryan Dunham

INTRODUCTION

Have you ever wondered why an all-knowing God ever asks a question? A God who sees the end from the beginning, knows every thought before it is spoken, and holds the universe in His hands has no lack of information. Yet, the pages of Scripture are filled with His questions. Lots of them. 620 of them, by my count. Admittedly, my list likely has flaws. Some questions are voiced through prophets, angels and theophany's. I have done my best to select only those clearly asked by God. There may be other questions that are up for debate. The appendix contains the list of the 622 questions.

I am not writing to engage in theological debate, but rather to consider the curious nature of a God who asks questions.

When God asks a question, it is never for His benefit – it is for ours. His questions are designed to make us pause, reflect, and wrestle with truth we might otherwise ignore. They uncover what is hidden, challenge what is assumed, and invite us into deeper relationship with Him.

This book explores ten of those questions. Each chapter begins with a story or personal reflection, followed by an examination of the context of the biblical question, its meaning to the original hearers, and its relevance for us today. The chapters are arranged chronologically as the questions appear in the Bible. You may read them in any order, as each chapter is designed to stand alone and provide a complete discussion of its question.

Along the way, you'll find the chapters begin with a story or personal reflection that may not, at first, seem directly related to the biblical question. I ask for your patience, as by the end of each chapter, the threads will come together and the relevance will be clear.

While not autobiographical, I share some very personal stories and struggles – things I would have hidden in the past; things I would have not wanted my friends to know, let alone published in a book. This is the freedom that Christ gives. As Paul said, I will boast all the more about my weaknesses... for when I am weak, then I am strong. His power is made perfect in weakness.

My hope is that as you read, you will not only examine the questions God asks but also allow them to examine you. Often the most significant obstacle in experiencing a closer relationship with God, living with more faith, less anxiety and more joy... is us. In a world where we long for answers, God gives us the gift of something better – the right question.

Happy reading.

TALKING SNAKES AND OUR MISTAKES

"BUT THE LORD GOD CALLED TO THE MAN AND SAID TO HIM, 'WHERE ARE YOU?'" GENESIS 3:9

As the old adage goes, "Familiarity breeds contempt." But perhaps it would be more accurate to say, "Familiarity renders things invisible."

There's actually a name for this phenomenon: the *Lullaby Effect*. It's what happens when something becomes so familiar, so often repeated, that we stop paying attention to it. Like a lullaby sung night after night, its meaning and force fade into the background, until it simply lulls us to sleep.

We've all experienced this. A well-worn story, a proverb, even a commercial jingle – at some point, the words and rhythms become automatic. Our brains go on autopilot. Instead of listening carefully, we coast, assuming there's nothing new to hear.

That's what makes the Lullaby Effect so dangerous. It doesn't deny the truth. It simply numbs us to it. Over time, we stop noticing *what has always been right in front of us.*

This is especially true with stories we think we know well. Consider *The Wizard of Oz, The Tortoise and the Hare,* or *Romeo and Juliet.* You could likely tell these stories quite accurately without ever opening a book. Because they are so familiar, when we hear them again, our brain quickly fills in the blanks and tunes out the details. We assume there's nothing left for us to learn.

And this is exactly the problem when we come to many stories in the Bible. Particularly with stories like the one that is the subject of this chapter: Adam and Eve. They're not just familiar; they're *too* familiar. We think, 'I already know this one,' and our minds go on vacation before God's Word has a chance to speak anything new.

I want to suggest: you don't know this story – at least, not as well as you think you do. My contention is that years of repetition and cognitive autopilot have left layers of mental dust, dulling our awareness. The Lullaby Effect has lulled us into thinking we've seen everything there is to see.

So here's my invitation: let's shake ourselves awake. Let's read this story as if for the first time, with eyes open and ears attentive, resisting the pull of the lullaby. If we do, I believe we'll discover things we've missed all along.

Are you willing to do that with me?

I thought you'd say yes.

Let's go.

❋

Since this is a book about the questions God asks, it only makes sense to begin with the very first one He poses in the Bible. In Genesis 3:9 we read, "...God called to the man, 'Where are you?'" As stated in the introduction, God is not asking this question because He does not know the answer. He is asking for the benefit of "the man." So... where is the man? In the verse just prior to the question we read:

> "And they heard the sound of the LORD God walking in the garden in the cool of the day, and the man and his wife hid themselves from the presence of the LORD God among the trees of the garden." Genesis 3:8

Where is the man? He (and his wife) are hiding. God being God, He already knows that they are not only hiding but also knows where. Adam (the man) clearly knows these things as well. So why is He asking the question? Is it possible that God is not asking about the physical location of Adam's body, but rather something else? If so, what is that something else? And what, if anything, does it say about us and our tendency to hide? Now before you begin thinking this book should really be titled, "Questions Bryan Asks," lets go back to the beginning of the story and see if we can find some answers.

Luckily, we are only three chapters into the whole Bible, so we don't have to go back very far. In Genesis chapter one, God creates the heavens and the earth and everything in them – plants, stars, the sun, the moon, animals, and finally man (I'll be using the word "man" a lot in this chapter – just know when I do, it almost always refers to "mankind," meaning both man and woman). It is important to note that when God creates man He notes something different about that creation that separates him from all other things He created:

> "So God created man in his own image, in the image of God he created him; male and female he created them."
> Genesis 1:27

This is what is referred to as the "Imago Dei," or the image of God. What is meant by the "image of God," and why is it important? We will get to that – for now, let's just note that this is unique to man.

Chapter one of Genesis is essentially an overview of the entire creation account – from nothing to everything that was created. Genesis chapter two is a more detailed account of the creation of Adam, the garden in which he was to live, his purpose for being in the garden, and one prohibition:

> "And the LORD God planted a garden in Eden, in the east, and there he put the man whom he had formed. And out of the ground the LORD God made to spring up every tree that is pleasant to the sight and good for food. The tree of life was in the midst of the garden, and the tree of the knowledge of good and evil." Genesis 2:8-9

> "The LORD God took the man and put him in the garden of Eden to work it and keep it. And the LORD God commanded the man, saying, 'You may surely eat of every tree of the garden, but of the tree of the knowledge of

good and evil you shall not eat, for in the day you eat of it you shall surely die.'" Genesis 2:15-16

Chapter two of Genesis concludes with God putting Adam to sleep, performing a little rib surgery, and creating Eve so that he would not be alone and to provide him some help with the working and keeping of the garden.

Now we come to the heart of our story – what is commonly known as "The Fall" – that ultimately leads to the first-recorded question God ever asked.

"Now the serpent was more crafty than any other beast of the field that the LORD God had made. He said to the woman, 'Did God actually say, "You shall not eat of any tree in the garden?"' Genesis 3:1

This is where the work of recognizing and restraining the Lullaby Effect begins. Before we jump to conclusions about what exactly is happening here based on what you have read or been told your whole life (i.e. the serpent is Satan who has arrived to tempt the humans to go against God's rules and thwart God's plan), – let's not let familiarity cloud our thought processes. Let's just take the story at face value and think through it.

The Old Testament was originally written in Hebrew. As not to lose anything in translation, we will be referring quite a bit to Hebrew words and their meanings. "Serpent" is the Hebrew word *nachash*. It is always translated as "serpent" or "snake". It doesn't mean anything else. Who created the serpent? We are told that,"...the serpent was more crafty *than any other beast of the field that the LORD God had made.*" (3:1)

God made all the beasts of the field – including this serpent. He also apparently made serpents "more crafty" than any other "beast of the field". What is translated as "more crafty" is the Hebrew word *arum*. This word can mean prudence, shrewdness, or (as in this verse) craftiness. *Arum* shows up eleven times in the Old Testament and is a nuanced word that can either be a positive or negative trait depending on context.

This serpent can also apparently talk – weird, right? What is even more odd is that the woman does not seem surprised by this fact at all. Why is that? Was this a regular occurrence? Since other animals speak in Scripture when God allows them to, I think it's at least worth considering that prior to the fall, all animals could speak – but I digress, that is for another book. (Did you feel any cognitive bias kick in when reading that last sentence?)

So we have this talking snake that is in a conversation with the woman, and to the characters in our story, this seems *totally normal*. So what does the snake say to her? He asks her a question about what God had prohibited the man and woman from doing. Before we get to the nature of the question, it's worth noting that the serpent is somehow aware that God has given the man and the woman at least one rule. So the serpent essentially asks, "Did God really say that you guys can't eat of any of the trees?" Whether the serpent has simply gotten bad information or is intentionally misconstruing and broadening the prohibition isn't actually clear.

> "And the woman said to the serpent, 'We may eat of the fruit of the trees in the garden, but God said, "You shall not eat of the fruit of the tree that is in the midst of the garden, neither shall you touch it, lest you die."'" Genesis 3:2-3

What is interesting here is how far off the woman's understanding of the prohibition is. Which tree was in the midst of the garden? Trick question – there are two of them: "...The tree of life was in the midst of the garden, and the tree of the knowledge of good and evil." (2:9) Which one is the woman speaking of? Does she know? Additionally, the woman adds to the prohibition by saying, "...neither shall you touch it..." which was not part of the original rule God put in place. Perhaps the woman's misunderstanding is forgivable because when the rule was given by God, she wasn't actually there. She had not been created yet. Presumably she had received the information about the prohibition from the man.

When my kids were toddlers, they were endlessly curious about almost everything, as most toddlers are. They often would reach up to the counter top to discover what their little fingers could grab, but their eyes could not see. Sometimes that would happen in the kitchen, where there are many dangerous or breakable things – knives, plates, appliances, etc. There is also the stove. When in use, the last place you would want precious little hands investigating is near the stovetop. So I would give them a stern warning anytime they were near the stove, even when it wasn't in use. "Don't touch the stove!" Now, was touching the stove a problem? Not always. In fact, not even most of the time. But because they could not yet understand when it was dangerous and when it wasn't, it was most safe to simply teach them to steer clear of it at all times.

I wonder if the man had a similar thought with the woman. "Don't eat from it... in fact, don't even touch the tree or you will die!"

"But the serpent said to the woman, 'You will not surely die. For God knows that when you eat of it your eyes will be opened, and you will be like God, knowing good and evil.'" Genesis 3:4

Before delving into what the serpent's goal is with this conversation, we need to address this concept of "the knowledge of good and evil." We first have the tree of the knowledge of good and evil from which they are not allowed to eat, and now the serpent explains that if they eat of this tree, they will possess this knowledge of good and evil. What exactly is the "knowledge of good and evil?"

It cannot be simply knowing right from wrong, for they already know that. The woman has just explained (though somewhat incorrectly) what they are allowed to do (what is right) and what they are not allowed to do (what is wrong). They understand the concept of what is right to do and what is wrong to do.

Besides, don't the words *right* and *wrong* have a different emotional temperature than *good* and *evil*? I don't know about you, but to me the words *good* and *evil* have a deeper level of quality and intensity than *right* and *wrong*.

One of the keys to understanding the phrase "knowing good and evil" is the Hebrew word for "knowing." It is the word *yada*. *Yada* is a very specific type of knowledge. This word is used in the very next chapter (4:1) to describe the relations that occurred between Adam and Eve to produce their son, Cain. While *yada* doesn't always mean sexual relations, it does mean intimate experiential knowledge. For example, I could write a biography about my three children – Courtney, Caleb and Rachel. I could detail all of their likes, dislikes, personality traits, quirks, and life events. If you read that biography, you would have an in-depth knowledge of my kids. However, that type of knowledge pales in comparison to how I know them – for I know them by experience. I've changed the diapers, rocked them to sleep, bandaged up skinned knees, helped with the homework, attended the recitals, held them when they cried, and taught them to drive. That is *yada*. Knowledge by experience.

In the case of the *yada* of good and evil – how do we obtain it?

There is a clear difference between *knowing* what is right and wrong and choosing *to do* what is right or what is wrong, and it's in the aftermath of the choice that we obtain the knowledge.

※

I will often go for a walk around my apartment complex during my lunch hour to break up the monotony of working from home. I'm usually in a bit of a time crunch to get in two miles, get home to make lunch, and then get back to work. About a month ago, I was nearing the end of one of those walks when I saw a car with a lady standing outside of it on her cell phone who looked like she might be having some trouble. It was a black Honda Accord, the nose of which was pointed towards a parking space, and the rest of it was hanging out in the street. It appeared to have simply stalled there. There was a look of concern on the lady's face as she spoke on the phone. My gut said, "You should see if she needs help." My mind immediately protested, "You have about 15 minutes to get back home, eat, and get to work – you don't have time for this! Besides, she is getting the help she needs – she is probably on the phone with someone who is coming to help... and do you think a woman who is alone, in a potentially vulnerable spot, wants some random guy to come try to help – she'll think you are some kind of creeper!"

Here I had a choice. I could stay focused on my goals, my day, my needs... or I could at least make an effort to put someone else before myself. I'm embarrassed to say that I had decided to look straight ahead and keep walking, but for some reason I stole one last glance at the woman and our eyes met. Something about the way she looked at me – my mind said, "Oh alright... go see if you can help." I walked over and asked, "Do you need any help?" She explained that she was coming back home, and the car just died right in this spot, and she didn't know what to do. She had called her husband, but he was at work, and it would take a while for him to arrive. I asked about common issues: was there gas in the tank? is the battery dead? will it start? etc. She explained that it would start, but the moment she gave it any gas, it would die. I had her start the car, put it in neutral, and I pushed the car while she steered it into the parking space. That was all she wanted. Her husband would be home in a couple of hours to figure out what to do, she just couldn't leave it partially blocking the street. Very relieved, she thanked me profusely and said, "You are an angel sent from God!"

I walked home on a cloud. I was elated. Her reaction made my day. I almost chose myself over this woman and her needs but ultimately chose to do the thing that I knew was right in this situation. What was the result? She got the help she needed, and I walked back home feeling like my life mattered today – even if it was such a simple task. There is a particular type of deep satisfaction and joy that is experienced only when you set aside your agenda to serve someone else. It feels like a tuning fork being struck in your soul. The emotional and spiritual payoff dwarfs the investment cost. It feels *right*. It feels *good*.

What I got to experience in that moment was a result of choosing to do what was right.

That is what is meant by the knowledge of good.

What about the knowledge of evil?

I have four siblings: 1 sister and 3 brothers. That sounds like a full house growing up, but because of the time between our births, I mostly grew up around just one brother – Chuck. Chuck and I are 1 1/2 years apart. Chuck really got on my nerves. A lot. Chuck's skin was pasty white with lots of freckles and tight, afro-like red curly hair. Plus he was a big nerd. He was super-smart and didn't hesitate to use that to his advantage. One such way he would accomplish this would be by using words I didn't understand, like "spasm." He would use that word as my nickname. The way he would say it – with additional emphasis on drawing out the "s" sound at the beginning and the "mmm" sound at the end instantly took me to a DEFCON 1 annoyance level. I'd walk into a room, and he would spit out, "Hey sssss-PAZ-mmmm..." There was a day we were getting along ok and playing badminton in our driveway. During a pause in the action, I asked him what a spasm was (I genuinely wanted to know and wasn't smart enough to look in a dictionary). Seeing an opportunity, his eyes lit up, and a non-symmetrical smile slowly spread across his face. He pursed his thin lips and croaked, "Mmmmm mhhhhh... (like he was tasting a deliciously rich cake) well...many people have ssssPAZmmmsss at nighttime... they can't control them... men and women both ssssPAZmmm. You ARE a ssssPAZmmm!"

If I told you the awful things my juvenile brain wanted to do to him in that moment, you'd probably stop reading this book, so I'll spare you – however, opportunity came knocking.

One day when I was about 8 years old, we were in the garage of our home working on our bicycles. A few days prior, while swimming at a neighbor's pool, Chuck forgot to put on sunscreen. The intense Texas summer sun had barbequed that aforementioned pale skin. So much so that he had serious blisters all across the top of both shoulders. That day, our mom had spread aloe vera across those blisters, and Chuck wasn't wearing a shirt. I was trying to air up the tires on my bike and was having trouble getting the hose connection to stay on the tire stem. Chuck hissed out, "That's not how you do it... ssssPAZmmm..."

As my annoyance edged towards a low level of rage, I looked up just as Chuck was turning his back to me. At that moment, the sunlight coming into the garage was falling across his shoulders. I noticed those blisters. How those full, red, fluid-filled bubbles of skin glistened with the aloe vera on them. I wanted to pop them. I wanted him to feel the pain. In fractions of a second, I imagined the deep satisfaction my soul would feel at such action.

In this moment, the right thing to do would be to swallow my pride, keep my mouth shut, and just go inside the house. Even at 8 I knew this. What did I do? I got up, moved quickly towards Chuck while his back was turned, raised both arms high above my head, leaped in the air for maximum force, and brought both of my hands down hard – slapping each shoulder with as much force as I could generate. I felt the awful wetness of blisters popping, the goopy aloe vera, the heat of his skin, and the mild sting in my hands due to the force of the contact. Chuck let out a yelp – a painful cry. The type of sorry, sickening sound that my 8-year-old ears had never before heard.

Instead of feeling satisfaction, I felt something else entirely. Nearly instantly I felt shocked that I did this to my brother. A deep, remorseful hollowness. It felt like I had seriously violated our relationship. It felt *wrong*. It felt *evil*. It was the first time in my life I can recall feeling so awful about my actions. What had I done?

That is what is meant by the knowledge of evil.

In one moment, I had the knowledge of right from wrong. In the next, I chose the wrong, and then I obtained the knowledge of evil – I came to know it by experience. I did the deed, received the consequences, and now had the terrible, intimate, experiential knowledge of committing acts I knew were wrong to begin with.

Of course, his cries brought my mother running out to the garage–who quickly called for my father. Exactly what happened next is hard to recall – it involved a lot of yelling and a belt to my backside – but the rest is lost to some type of dissociative amnesia often experienced by those who commit crimes of passion.

Take a moment and recall a time when you really blew it. Where you clearly knew what was right and what was wrong, yet you still chose the wrong. What was that experience like for you? How did it make you feel?

The bigger question is why did you do it? Why did I do it? Let's see if the story in Genesis 3 holds any answers for us.

❂

Let's return again to verse 4:

> "But the serpent said to the woman, 'You will not surely die. For God knows that when you eat of it your eyes will be opened, and you will be like God, knowing good and evil.'" Genesis 3:4

What is the serpent's goal in this conversation? That depends on who or what you think the serpent is. Orthodox Christianity teaches that this serpent has been embodied by Satan, and this story is about Satan tempting Eve by questioning God and His goodness. This verse is traditionally interpreted as Satan (via the serpent) throwing shade on God: "God is lying to you – you aren't going to die. In fact, God doesn't want you to eat of the fruit of the tree because it will make you like Him. He is holding out on you. He is trying to limit your experience of life."

I agree that Satan is the enemy of our soul and his tactics absolutely align with the traditional interpretation of this verse. Lying is his native tongue. He will tempt us. He twists God's word like a pretzel. He wants you to disobey God's clear commands.

However, none of that is explicit in this story – it has to be arrived at through interpretation of other Scriptures. Remember that we are setting aside familiarity bias (the story we are familiar with)? So let's keep seeing this verse as if it were the first time we ever read it and simply take it at face value.

What if the snake is just... being a snake?

Let me ask- what is the difference between humans and animals?

Secular and humanistic philosophies would say, "nothing – we are no different than the animals, just more evolved."

Many Christians would argue against that thought with Genesis 2:7 that says, "...then the LORD GOD formed the man of the dust from the ground and breathed into his nostrils the breath of life, and the man became a living creature." While this intimate description of man's creation is unique, the substance of the act is not; we read a few verses later in Genesis 2:19, "Now out of the ground the LORD God had formed every beast of the field and every bird of the heavens...". Earlier in the creation account we also read, "And to every beast of the earth and to every bird of the heavens and to everything that creeps on the earth, everything that has the breath of life, I have given every green plant for food." A little later in Genesis, when Noah builds the ark before the great flood, we read, "Pairs of all creatures that have the breath of life in them came to Noah and entered the ark." (Genesis 7:15) So we see that neither being formed from the ground, not having the breath of life makes man unique.

If there is a difference, what is it?

We mentioned it earlier – the Imago Dei – the image of God. God is very explicit that man is made in His image and His likeness, and nothing else in creation is. So what does that mean? Does it mean that we physically resemble God – God has two hands, two feet, two arms, two legs, a torso, and a head? This can't be right, for we are told that God is Spirit (John 4:24). So how do we resemble God, and how is that different from the animals?

Let's come at this from a different angle. Can geese fly north in the winter? Can roosters silence themselves at dawn? Can spiders decide not to spin webs or choose not to eat what gets trapped in them? Of course not. Animals are not making these decisions, they are operating off of instinct. There is no option for them to do otherwise.

That doesn't mean animals don't have intelligence. Bottlenose dolphins can recognize themselves in mirrors, cooperate in hunting, and can understand human hand signals. Chimpanzees use tools, solve complex problems, and communicate with gestures and sounds. Octopuses can solve mazes, open jars, and escape enclosures.

While that is all really cool, we aren't granting animals the right to run for public office anytime soon.

What if this story is less about Satan wrecking the game plan of God and more about what distinguishes humans from animals?

Again, taking this story at face value, the snake is just a snake and knows no other way to operate than off of instinct: "If the tree has good fruit on it, and I want it, I will eat it – verbal prohibitions be damned – no questions asked. You should try it." The snake is not going to rationally consider the impact of its actions on itself or its environment. It isn't going to take time to consider whether it's wise to eat the fruit or not. Those are things that humans do. Animals do not have that ability. It is not possible for a snake to be a human.

But is it possible for a human to be a snake?

Here we have arrived at one of the most significant differences between humans and animals – the capacity for moral choice. There is no capacity for moral choice when it comes to an animal. They act purely by instinct.

You and I might call them desires. We as humans can discern the difference between what we *want* to do, and what we *should* do. We have the choice to do either.

And perhaps for the first time in her life, Eve is confronted with this choice:

> "So when the woman saw that the tree was good for food, and that it was a delight to the eyes, and that the tree was to be desired to make one wise, she took of its fruit and ate..." Genesis 3:6

We are given an intimate view of how Eve is thinking – how she is talking to herself about this situation.

Pause for a moment and let's insert ourselves in the story: when we desire something we should not have, what kind of self-talk do we use to persuade ourselves it's ok to have it? God has called this fruit forbidden – but Eve has now talked herself into seeing it as "good."

The momentum of her reasoning fueled by her desire rapidly picks us speed as she sees it will not only satisfy her hunger ("good for food"), but it is also physically attractive ("delight to the eyes"), and it would give her knowledge she had yet to obtain ("was to be desired to make one wise"). Confronted with choosing what she wants over God's clear command, she makes a snake-like move and obeys her instincts. "She saw... she took... she ate..." Eve has made the decision that she will decide for herself what is good, and no longer depend on God for that guidance. She chooses her desire over God's directive.

❀

For all the complexity in the details of the Bible, the overall scheme is really quite simple. Humans are frequently presented with two options – God's way or their own way:

> Moses told Israel:
> "I call heaven and earth to witness against you today, that I have set before you life and death, blessing and curse. Therefore choose life, that you and your offspring may live, loving the Lord your God, obeying his voice and holding fast to him, for he is your life and length of days, that you may dwell in the land that the Lord swore to your fathers, to Abraham, to Isaac, and to Jacob, to give them." Deuteronomy 30:18-20

> Joshua challenged them:
> *"Choose this day whom you will serve... But as for me and my house, we will serve the LORD."* Josh. 24:15.

Elijah confronted them:
"How long will you go limping between two opinions? If the LORD is God, follow him; but if Baal, then follow him." 1 Kings 18:21

Jesus pressed the same choice: treasure on earth or in heaven (Matt. 6:19–21), anxiety or trust (Matt. 6:31–33), self-preservation or self-denial (Mark 8:34–36).

The message is consistent and the choice is binary:

- Choose life or death.

- Serve God or other gods.

- Follow the LORD or idols.

- Seek heaven's treasure or earth's.

- Deny self or forfeit your soul.

While the choice is simple, the consequences are significant. So why is it so hard to consistently choose what is right? Our desires – the things we want – often war against the things we need. Scripture identifies this pull away from God's desires toward our own and often calls it "the world." It is not speaking of the physical earth but is used to identify a godless system of values, priorities, and desires that stand in opposition to God. For us humans, there are three primary areas in which we are tempted to adopt this value system of the world:

"Do not love the world or the things in the world... for all that is in the world – the desires of the flesh and the desires of the eyes and the pride of life – is not from the Father but is from the world." 1 John 2:15-16

Not ironically, Eve experiences all three of these – "she saw that it was good for food" (desires of the flesh) and a "delight to the eyes" (desire of the eyes) and "was to be desired to make one wise" (pride of life).

The above verse in first John states that while there are desires that are from the world, it also implies there are desires that are from God. God has given us the basic desire (or instinct, if you will) for self-preservation, hunger, thirst, and desire for community, spiritual longing, and to worship (among many others). We might also call desire, "passion." What's more, our passions are the fuel and spice of our lives. They are what produces the horsepower that drives us to achieve, to create, to improve, and to experience.

So if following the flow of our passions can lead to so much good, how could it be wrong? Because unbridled passions can also lead to tremendous pain and destruction. Howard Hughes' passion for ambition and perfection that led to dramatic fortune and fame, ultimately left him a profoundly isolated recluse, emaciated and addicted to morphine. Marilyn Monroe's passion to find love and validation led to unchecked relationships, substance abuse, and death by overdose. Hitler's passion for returning Germany to greatness on the world stage led to the murder of millions of Jews.

Passion without parameters does not lead to freedom but to ruin.

Of course – God knows this. God does not want to extinguish our passions. He gave them to us in the first place. He wants to provide direction to them. His commands harness and focus our passions toward positive, worthwhile, productive ends. God-directed passions lead to holy outcomes.

As David said, "I run in the path of your commands, for you have set my heart free." (Psalm 119:32)

God's instructions, rightly considered, bring freedom – not limitations.

One of the great questions of life is: will we seek to fulfill our desires in a way that honors God's instructions, or will we seek our own path of fulfillment? Will we, like Eve, take the reins and decide for ourselves what is good and what is evil? There are consequences to both.

❋

Picking up where we left off:

> "...she took of its fruit and ate, and she also gave some to her husband who was with her, and he ate. Then the eyes of both were opened, and they knew that they were naked. And they sewed fig leaves together and made themselves loincloths." Genesis 6b-7

Eve's desire to fulfill her needs on her own overcomes her knowledge of what is right, she takes the fruit, eats it, and gives some to Adam who was with her.

As an aside, when I was younger, I always pictured the serpent approaching Eve while she was alone, and that is how the serpent could get away with being wrong about God's command and how Eve could incorrectly explain what she understood about that same command – for if Adam were with her, surely he would have corrected her! Interestingly, when the serpent uses the word "you" in the dialogue with the woman, this is plural in Hebrew, indicating he is speaking to more than just Eve. And now we read in this verse Adam is standing there with her as she eats, in all his passive glory, and then eats some of the fruit right after her. To the men reading this – our instinctive bent toward passivity when it comes to leading in a marriage and in a home is nothing new. It began with the first man. That is not an excuse for this behavior – for it goes against God's order – I just want you to know that you are not alone.

Immediately we read, "the eyes of both were opened, and they knew they were naked." Suddenly, whatever they thought they were going to gain by obeying their desire turns out to be something very different. We know this because the next thing they do is cover up the visual evidence of their transgression: "And they sewed fig leaved together and made themselves loincloths." (3:7)

> "And they heard the sound of the LORD God walking
> in the garden in the cool of the day, and the man and his
> wife hid themselves from the presence of the LORD God
> among the trees of the garden. But the LORD God called
> to the man and said to him, 'Where are you?' And he said,
> 'I heard the sound of you in the garden, and I was afraid,
> because I was naked, and I hid myself.'" Genesis 3:8-10

Now they have come to know good and evil *by experience*. Far from simply knowing right from wrong, they have chosen the wrong and are now experiencing the consequences. And thus begins the instinct we all have, even to this day, when we do something we know we shouldn't have done – when we, like Adam and Eve, come to the knowledge of good and evil. The shame and fear we feel causes us to cover and hide. We delete the text stream, the browser history, or the call log. We stop returning texts, don't answer the phone, and stop looking at email. It's a return to childhood where we would cover our eyes when we did something wrong because "if I can't see them, they can't see me."

Unfortunately, that's not the end of Adam and Eve's attempts to distance themselves from accepting responsibility for their actions.

> "He (God) said, 'Who told you that you were naked? Have you eaten of the tree of which I commanded you not to eat?' The man said, 'The woman whom you gave to be with me, she gave me fruit of the tree and I ate.' Then the LORD God said to the woman, 'What is this that you have done?' The woman said, 'The serpent deceived me, and I ate.'" Genesis 3:11-13

Ahh yes – the final desperate attempt we all employ to justify our disobedience – blame shifting. And to whom are they shifting blame?

"The woman you gave me..."

"The serpent deceived me..."

"Look God – if you hadn't given me that woman... if you hadn't created serpents..."

We might say: It wasn't my fault! It was my parents. It's just the culture of the times. I was just so stressed out. I wouldn't have done it, if they wouldn't have (fill in the blank).

We blame shift because we don't want to face the idea that we did *that thing* because somewhere down deep inside, *we wanted to.* That's a difficult reality to face, especially when the consequences are so devastating.

So now, finally, let's answer the question that is the focus of this chapter. God asks Adam: "Where are you?"

Adam (and Eve) is lost. Not physically of course; but spiritually, emotionally. They are hiding in fear and shame because they followed their desire to choose for themselves what was right and wrong and violated the most important relationship in their lives. Internally they are in that barren, cold wilderness where they feel helpless and alone with no clear way out of the mess they have created. If you've lived long enough, you've been there, too. I have. You may be there now.

God's question to Adam is to get him to realize where he is spiritually – actively creating separation between himself and God and attempting to maintain the distance by hiding from Him – when the only way out of his predicament is the exact opposite of his instinct – to confess his transgression and return to God. To seek Him and not hide from Him.

❂

May I ask: Where are you? (by "you" I mean the one reading these words right now)

Whose kingdom are you choosing to be a part of? One of God's making or one of your own? Are your passions self-directed or God directed?

Where are you?

It's a question I frequently ask myself... "Where am I?"

Though I still stumble, I'm learning - imperfectly - to live surrendered. I still feel the tug toward following my own desires, propping up my own pride, leaning into instinct instead of obedience. But I've also found a quiet grace in laying down my agenda each morning, and in trusting my desires to a father who knows them better than I do. And when I forget, when I fall, I'm reminded - he hasn't gone anywhere. He still asks the question: Where are you?

It's not the voice of an accuser, but of a loving creator, walking in the cool of the day, looking for His children. Not to shame, but to invite. Not to scold, but to restore.

So maybe today, instead of hiding or hustling, we can pause long enough to hear His voice and let the question linger: where are you?

Not just, what have you done? But where are you - really?

Maybe that's where healing begins.

Maybe that's where the story starts to change...

CHAPTER TWO

WHAT WE FAIL TO GOVERN, WILL GOVERN US

"THE LORD SAID TO CAIN, 'WHY ARE YOU ANGRY, AND WHY HAS YOUR FACE FALLEN?'"

I shared a story in the last chapter about my brother Chuck. While he won't be making an appearance in every chapter, he will be again in this one. As I mentioned, I found Chuck intensely annoying. Partially because he seemed immune from what I felt was the ever present weight of peer pressure. He definitely walked to the beat of his own drummer.

If you are old enough, you will recall the fad of cuffing or tight-rolling your jeans. If you are too young, or simply don't remember, this was the process of taking the bottom of your jean pant leg, pinching a portion of it between your thumb and fingers, pulling it outward until is was taut, then folding it over and wrapping it around your ankle. You then proceeded to "cuff", or roll up the fold in typically two neat rolls. This created a tapering effect for your jeans. When I was in junior high, all the cool people did this. Which meant I did this. Not because I was necessarily cool, but I was desperately trying to be.

My brother felt no such need. While he appreciated the tapered look of the jeans, he saw no point in go through the process of tight-rolling them. In his eyes it was much more efficient to simply take one of mom's diaper pins, fold the pant leg over the bottom and pin them into place. So he had that tapered look, but also had a diaper pin glinting off of the bottom of his jeans in the sunlight. So sad to say as an adult, but I was not only embarrassed to be around him – I was embarrassed for him. I didn't know if it was naivete to what cool really was, or an intentional flaunting of the social fabric of kid-dom. I watched the kids at school point and snicker at his jeans. His apparent complete imperviousness to the ridicule for some reason made me even more annoyed.

In those days, when I got off the bus and walked in the door of my house there were two questions my mother always asked: 1.) "How was school?" and 2.) "Do you have any homework?" To which my answers were always "good" and "no". I never, ever had homework. At least none that I admitted to. I learned long ago that I wouldn't be allowed to play video games, go to a friends house, or go outside and shoot hoops until I had all my homework done. Thus, I never had any. At times my mom would ask me with a raised eyebrow "How is it that you never seem to have homework??" To which I provided the universal kid reply of "I don't know" and would then attempt to leave the room as quickly as possible to end what felt like a brewing interrogation. Mostly I either never did my homework and took zero's or I scratched something together on the bus to school in the mornings. I didn't get bad grades – mostly A's and B's with the occasional C. Being 13, my thought was I just didn't have to try hard to make that happen, so why should I?

My brother on the other hand, would come home and immediately go up to his room to do two things: 1.) His homework (which he always seemed to have) and 2.) Practice his trumpet (because, of course, he was in band). He would be slaving away in his room from the moment he got home until my mom called us for dinner. I would be outside for hours, goofing around in the yard, visiting friends or shooting hoops in our driveway. If I was around the house I would often hear him blaring away on his trumpet. His bedroom window was on the second floor just above our driveway. Sometimes, when I was shooting hoops, he would open the window and hiss "Hey sssPAZmmm... you sure are missing a lot of shots..." or he would take the mute out of his trumpet (that muffled the sound) and blare out a few shrill notes through the screen in an attempt to make my play less enjoyable. He seemed to me like a modern day Quasimodo, shunned by society and locked in his tower high above. The only member of the fellowship of diaper-penned pants. This was the enigma that was my brother. I had long since given up trying to figure him out.

In Chapter one, I mentioned that I have four siblings – three brothers and a sister. My sister Margie is the oldest, Jeff is about 1 1/2 years younger than her and 13 years older than me. My youngest brother Chris is 12 years younger than me. By the time I was 6 both Margie and Jeff were out of the house on their own, and Chris wasn't born yet, so it was really just me and Chuck growing up.

My father was a quick-tempered alcoholic who held absolute power in our home. He often exercised that power in what felt like an oppressive and, at times, cruel way. I was a bit of an independent spirit and needless to say there was a lot of friction between my father and I. We would frequently argue, and when it got really heated I could see the fear rising in my mothers eyes. When the tension would subside, more than once my mother would pull me aside and say "Do you want to know how I've gotten along with your father all these years? I do whatever he says to do, and I do it immediately. If you would just do that, you will never have a problem with your father." Hearing this from my mother made me seethe with anger even more towards my father. My mom was the most gentle, loving and spiritual person I have ever known, even to this day. That my dad would routinely treat her as his doormat, and that she had accepted this as her role in their relationship angered and dumfounded me.

For whatever reason, my father seemed to scrutinize everything about me. I was a tall, lanky and skinny teenager. I was so thin that sometimes when my father was physically near me he would chortle "Hey! Don't stab me with those elbows!", chuckling as he walked away. My father didn't like the shape my shoulders would take when sitting or walking and would look at me and growl "Shoulders back, boy!" He said this so frequently he just shortened to a terse "SB boy!" He would do this at home and in public, and when in public would say this noticeably louder in what felt like an attempt to not only embarrass me, but to make a display of his dominance. My reaction was exaggerated obedience – I would quickly pop to attention, throwing back my shoulders as far as they would go. It would have the effect of making my back so straight you could have ironed clothes on it. In this way I was being obedient in a way that felt like disobedience and a rejection of his command. For all my dad's faults, I clearly didn't do much to build a bridge for a relationship . I don't recall him ever using my actual name. He referred to me as either "boy", "dummy" or "damnit". Whenever we would pass a street sign that said "Dip" (indicating an unusually low point in the road was upcoming), he would snicker "Hey boy! Look – your name is on that sign!" followed by a giggling fit so serious it would cause his shoulders to shake.

At 14 years old I was feeling the tension of not liking my father (I would have even used the word "hate" at the time), while in the same moment, desperately wanting to please him. The anger I felt at my father's seeming rejection of me I used for fuel in athletics. I excelled at sports. To the outsider looking in it may have appeared that I was somewhat naturally gifted in that area, but the reality was the situation with my father drove me to want to be better than anyone one else at what I did athletically. I chose basketball as my sport and would spend hours in the driveway, working on my shot, working on certain moves, in my own world of make believe. One day, I was taking out the trash and saw my basketball sitting in the flower bed. Even though I was barefoot, since I was only supposed to be outside for a few seconds, I decided to pick up that ball and get in a few free throws. When practicing, my concentration was so intense, I would often lose track of time. Two hours later I wrapped up this solo practice session because it was time for bed. When I got inside I saw that I had blood blisters on my feet from not wearing shoes. That was how obsessed I was. I fantasized that one day I would hit the winning shot or get an athletic scholarship or go on to play professionally and somewhere along the way I would finally earn my father's love. Truth is, if I could just get his acceptance it felt like that would have been enough. I did well at basketball. By my second year playing I was starting on the 8th grade team. By the end of my senior year I was voted MVP of our team, MVP of our district, was on the Texas All-Star North team, and was an All-State forward. Yet, each time he came to watch me play I never heard, "Well done" or "I'm proud of you". In fact, on the best night of my high school career, I was flirting with the all-time single game school scoring record. I missed it by four points.

I finished the game with 38 points, 18 rebounds and 4 blocked shots. When I climbed in the cab of my dad's pick up to go home he said "Just couldn't get that record, could you? You know the reason you didn't was..." and he proceeded to detail every major flaw he thought he saw in my game that night. I felt like I was suffocating. I needed his love and acceptance, yet despite my best performance, I couldn't obtain it.

Additionally, the way my father treated my brother Chuck was fuel to the fire. My father seemed to admire Chuck. It is hard to describe, but just the way he looked at Chuck seemed as though he was proud of him. I always thought it was just because he wasn't around our father long enough for my father to lay into him. As I mentioned, on school days Chuck stayed in his room, and on weekends he was usually working (Chuck got a job at 15 – as early as he could get one). He always called Chuck by his name when he spoke to him – that or "Chuke" – which has a long back story, but suffice it to say was delivered in a tone of endearment. One day, I came to understand why my father seemed to favor Chuck over me. I don't recall the exact topic, but I was again arguing with my father and finally let loose with all of my suppressed emotion and vitriol over his inability to be pleased with me, when he was so easily pleased with Chuck. My dad stopped yelling, paused and looked at me with intense curiosity – as though he was astonished that I didn't know the answer to that question. He said, "Are you that much of a dummy? Chuck tries hard. He works hard to get grades that you can skate by and get. He is first chair in band because he works so hard to have it and keep it. He has a job where he works long hours and saves his money. You are lazy. You should be more like Chuck." As he walked off. I felt like I had been punched in the gut. There it was. What my 14 year old ears heard was interpreted by my brain as "The Bryan you are is not good enough. You are just a dummy... a dip. If you want to please me, you need to be like your brother."

Feeling the frustration of knowing I could never be Chuck, I took the anger I was feeling toward my father, and redirected toward my brother. He was the measuring stick that was causing me so much emotional pain. It was his fault.

❖

"The LORD said to Cain, 'Why are you angry, and why has your face fallen?'" Genesis 4:6

The question God asks in this chapter is just one chapter in Genesis away from what we covered in chapter 1, and like that chapter (and every other one in this book) we have to get the backstory to truly understand why God is asking what He is asking.

To catch us up from the last chapter, due to their disobedience, Adam and Eve have been kicked out of the Garden of Eden. They have now made their home outside of its confines and begin to have a family. Their firstborn they name Cain and the second born is named Abel. We are not told how much younger Abel is than Cain. What does the text tell us about this duo?

"...Now Abel was a keeper of the sheep, and Cain was a worker of the ground." Genesis 4:2

Though the order is reversed here, do the words "keep" and "work" ring any bells? In Genesis 2:15 God places the Adam in the garden "to work it and to keep it." This seems to be the first human attempts at delegation and specialization. Cain will "work" and Adam will "keep". Even more specific, Cain will work "the ground" and Abel will keep "the sheep."

So it seems Abel is a shepherd, and Cain is type of farmer. On the surface this is pretty straight forward, but sometimes looking at the underlying Hebrew words can provide a deeper view into what we are reading. As far as Abel goes, the Hebrew word for "keeper" is the word *roeh* and means to tend, to feed or to associate with as a friend. There is a friendly, caring, perhaps even happy connotation to this description of Abel's job. It seems to describe not only *what* he does, but *the way in which he goes about it* – his attitude about it. When it comes to Cain, the Hebrew word for "worker" is *avad*, which means to work in any sense, but carries with it the connotation of servitude; even bondage – as in slavery. I wonder if the text is giving us a view into the attitude of how Cain sees his occupation.

> "In the course of time Cain brought to the LORD an offering of the fruit of the ground..." Genesis 4:3

This is the first record of anyone ever bringing an offering to God, and its Cain that is doing it. There is no record of any command of God or of Adam to bring an offering at this point. Taking the text at face value, this seems to be Cain's decision – a voluntary gift from the produce of the ground for which he was responsible. Keep in mind that just because it is the first time *we are told* an offering was brought, doesn't mean this was *the first time it occurred.*

"In the course of time" is "vague and may imply that the practice of giving offerings was customary for the brothers, perhaps learned from Adam."[1]

> "...and Abel also brought of the firstborn of his flock and
> of their fat portions." Genesis 4:4a

This Hebrew word for "also" is *gam*. It occurs two times in the text prior to this verse. First when Eve eats of the forbidden fruit and we read "she *also* gave some to her husband". The second occurrence is when God is discussing the reason for the man needing to leave the garden in Genesis 3:22: "...lest he reach out his hand and take *also* of the tree of life and eat, and live forever...". In both instances thus far it indicates two separate actions that happen in succession, right after the other. Eve eats and immediately gives some *also;* the couple must be removed from the garden lest the man may take and *also* eat.

It seems likely that Cain makes the decision to provide God an offering, and Abel thinks this is a great idea and right on the heels of Cain's offering, Abel makes his.

While the text offers no description of the quality of Cain's offering, it does with Abel's. Abel brings the "firstborn" of his flock of sheep (the firstborn echoes of a critical theme threaded throughout the Old Testament pertaining to sacrifice, redemption and God's covenant with Israel). We also read that Abel brought "...of their fat portions." This is one word in Hebrew: *Cheleb*. *Cheleb* can mean the fat portion of a piece of meat, but used figuratively it can mean the "finest or choicest

---

1. NAC, Genesis, Matthews

part." Abel's offering is top shelf. While that is great for Abel, is the text also trying to communicate that Cain's offering was lesser quality? Perhaps, but that is an argument from silence for we are told nothing of the quality of Cain's offering.

> "And the LORD had regard for Abel and his offering, but
> for Cain and his offering he had no regard." Genesis 4:5

The word that is translated as "regard" is the Hebrew word *shahah*. It "describes an act of turning the face or the inner attention toward someone or something. In Scripture it is never a casual glance; it signals decisive regard, whether in gracious favor, desperate appeal, or stern refusal."[2]

Mostly I learned through Sunday school lessons and sermons on this topic that it was the offering itself that was the issue. Abel's offering was better – of highest quality. Cain just didn't bring his best stuff. He was holding out on God and keeping the best for himself. That interpretation leads to a great lesson on how we should always bring our best to God, no matter what we are doing or giving. However, is that the best or even the most straight forward reading?

Notice that the text doesn't say He had regard for "Abel's offering" but no regard for "Cain's offering". It says that God "...had regard for Abel *and his offering*", "...but for Cain *and his offering* he had no regard." It lists the person and their offering separately.

Is there something about the *individual* for which God has regard that is over and above the physical sacrifice each brings?

---

2. https://biblehub.com/hebrew/8159.htm

Let's look to scripture to see what we can learn about sacrifices to God. Up until this point in the story, there have been no commanded sacrifices and no rules in regard to how those sacrifices should be offered. Later in the Old Testament, in the book of Leviticus, there are 5 primary types of sacrifices that are prescribed. Those 5 were: burnt offerings (Leviticus 1); grain offerings (Leviticus 2); peace offerings (Leviticus 3); sin offerings (Leviticus 4 and 5); and trespass offerings (Leviticus 5). These offerings were central to Israel's worship of God and a means of maintaining their relationship with Him.

Ok. So we know the types of sacrifices required, and a reading of Leviticus would provide the reason a person would use a particular type of sacrifice and how to perform it. Are there any other verses that inform what God is desiring related to sacrifice beyond just the manner and act itself? There are. And these verses seem to subordinate the importance of the sacrifice itself to something God values more:

> "If I (God) were hungry, I would not tell you, for the world and its fullness are mine. Do I eat the flesh of bulls or drink the blood of goats? Offer to God a sacrifice of thanksgiving, and perform your vows to the Most High..."
> Psalm 50:12-14

> "Has the LORD as great delight in burnt offerings and sacrifices, as in obeying the voice of the LORD? Behold, to obey is better than sacrifice, and to listen than the fat of rams." 1 Samuel 15:22

"For you will not delight in sacrifice, or I would give it; you
will not be pleased with a burnt offering. The sacrifices
of God are a broken spirit; a broken and contrite heart, o
God, you will not despise." Psalm 51:16-17

"When you come to appear before me (God), who has
required of you this trampling of my courts? Bring no
more vain offerings; incense is an abomination to me.
New moon and Sabbath and the calling of convocations
– I cannot endure iniquity and solemn assembly. Your
new moons and your appointed feasts my soul hates; they
have become a burden to me; I am weary of bearing them.
When you spread out your hands, I will hide my eyes
from you; even though you make many prayers, I will
not listen; your hands are full of blood. Wash yourselves,
make yourselves clean; remove the evil of your deeds from
before my eyes; cease to do evil, learn to do good; seek
justice, correct oppression; bring justice to the fatherless,
plead the widow's cause." Isaiah 1:14-20

Is there something God values more than the religious activity of the
sacrifices He himself commanded? Yes – according to these verses they
are: thanksgiving, obedience, and a repentant heart that is reflected in a
life of goodness, justice and mercy. God in effect is saying "I don't even
want your sacrifices if your heart and life are not in the right place."

Is this the reason Cain is in the predicament he is in?

We saw earlier how the Hebrew language may give us some insight
into the internal world of Cain and Abel in relation to their vocation:

Abel seeing himself as a companion and caregiver to the sheep, and Cain seeing himself as a slave to the ground. Have you ever had a job where you felt more like a slave than an employee? How was your attitude at that time?

What has been going on inside of Cain begins to surface when he experiences the rejection of God.

"So Cain was very angry, and his face fell." Genesis 4:5b

This Hebrew word that is translated as "angry" is *charah* – which means to "wax hot" – you and I might say "burn with anger." He isn't merely disgruntled- Cain is seething with anger, and it is written all over his face.

"The LORD said to Cain, 'Why are you angry, and why has your face fallen?'"

Thus God asks the question that is the subject of this chapter. Why are you angry?

We have already seen that what prompts Cain's outrage here is that "...for Cain and his offering he had no regard." God doesn't just reject Cain's offering – he is also rejects *Cain himself.*

I believe scripture is telling us that Cain's mistake is not the quality of the sacrifice, but the quality of his attitude. God wants nothing to do with religious sacrifice, even the finest gift, if it is not accompanied by the right heart posture.

"If you do well, will you not be accepted? And if you do
not do well, sin is crouching at the door. Its desire is to
have you, but you must rule over it." Genesis 4:7

In the same breath God gives Cain both a way out and a warning.

The way out – the way for Cain and his offering to be accepted – is
simply to "do well". What does it mean to do well in God's view? "He
(God) has shown you, O man, what is good. And what does the LORD
require of you but to act justly, to love mercy, and to walk humbly with
your God?" (Micah 6:6-8) God is interested in humility and ethical
living over rote religious activity. Mindless and heartless ritual is of zero
interest to God, will not be acceptable to Him, and is a waste of our time.

And if Cain does not do well? Sin is "crouching at the door." Sin is
lurking around the door to Cain's heart and is waiting to pounce. Cain's
angry attitude could eventually open the door to sin to stroll right in and
make itself at home. God lovingly warns Cain that he has the option to
"rule over it". Cain has a choice here. He can "do well", or he can "not
do well". He can "rule over" his sinful desires, or he can give himself over
to them.

At this point in the story, God has moved beyond Cain's inadequate
attitude and highlights something that is even more important than
the rejected sacrifice – *What will he do with the resulting emotions that
accompany the rejection?*

Rejection is one of the most painful emotions we can experience
because it strikes at our deepest God-given need for connection and
belonging. It would be painful enough if he were rejected by his dad,
mom or brother. But this rejection is from God Himself.

God plainly tells Cain (and us), that sinful desires can be ruled, and
that we can do it – in fact that we must do it. This does not mean that

you will not have sinful desires – it just means that you do not have to give in to them. They do not have to rule you. However, that becomes increasingly challenging to do when strong emotions are involved, and Cain is steaming mad.

●

In psychology, anger is termed a "secondary emotion". This means is usually it doesn't arrive first, but follows on the heels of another emotion like fear, frustration, injustice or hurt. Because those emotions display our vulnerabilities, anger often quickly surfaces as a defense mechanism.

We experience this not only as individuals but as a collective.

When I was younger, I remember adults talking about the assassination of JFK. It always seemed to be accompanied by the phrase "I remember exactly where I was and what I was doing when I heard the news..." Almost as if time had stopped that day. It was a moment in time they could return to by simply being reminded of what occurred. I always thought that was adults just being dramatic and wanting to be a part of "the team".

Then, on the morning of September 11th, 2001 I was driving into an office where I worked as a financial advisor in Grapevine, Tx. I was just passing Grapevine Mills Mall and listening to sports radio on 1310 The Ticket. The show was "The Musers" and I recall in the middle of a segment discussing something about Oklahoma football, one of the hosts, George Dunham (no relation) blurted out "What the heck is going on at the World Trade Center?" Craig Miller (another host) said "Good God... smoke billowing out of the top 10-20 stories..." We would of course go on to learn the sickening truth that a highjacked plane had intentionally crashed into the North Tower, and was just the beginning of the worst terrorist attack in history on U.S. soil.

I now know exactly what those who remember the assassination of JFK were talking about. All I have to do is recall that day, and I remember everything about what was happening when I first heard that news.

The emotions I remember were first bewilderment – what was going on? Then it turned to sorrow and hurt. It wasn't long before anger took hold. I was feeling angry about the attack long before we even knew who was responsible. I think we all were.

Toby Keith penned and recorded "Courtesy of the Red, White and Blue (The Angry American)" and many of us sang along with fantasies of the righteous vengeance our military would rain down on those who were to blame.

We were hurt. We were angry. We wanted vengeance for those that were killed and the horrible images that remained seared in our minds – the planes being swallowed up by those massive towers, the balls of flame shooting out the other side, the helpless people jumping from windows, the smoke rushing through the streets as the buildings failed, and finally the twisted iron remnants of the fallen towers with an American flag sticking up out of the heap of metal that once were two of the largest and most iconic buildings in the world.

It was a day I will never forget. I can still recall the feelings of shock and sadness. I even got a little misty-eyed typing it.

Do you ever wonder what was done with all of that scrap steel from those buildings?

On November the 7th, 2009 the USS New York was commissioned into service by the U.S. Navy. It is designed as an amphibious assault transport – it will take marines and their equipment where it needs to go for warfare. It was built with 7 1/2 tons of steel salvaged from the

World Trade Center. It has a large emblem on the hull of the ship that depicts a phoenix rising from flames with an image of the twin towers in the background, and the words "NEVER FORGET" across the bottom of the image. We took the wreckage of our hurt, melted it down, created a warship out of it, and affixed an emblem that said "never forget".

For all of the patriotic feelings this evokes in me, it also provides an apt metaphor and a personification of what God is warning Cain about in our story.

When we experience significant hurt, we look around at the wreckage of our heart in pain and confusion. Many times we internalize that pain, ruminating on what happened, why it happened and who did it to us. Then we weaponize that pain, stamp it "never forget" and use it to assault others, most of which had nothing to do with the origination of our hurt. As they say: Hurt people, hurt people.

Anger itself is not a sin in the Bible; but vengeance is.

❁

"Cain spoke to Abel his brother. And when they were in
the field, Cain rose up against his brother and killed him."
Genesis 4:8

Like the animals (and his mother before him), Cain obeys his desires, not God's directive, chooses the wrong over the right, and slays Abel.

Cain has internalized his rejection, weaponized his pain and it decides to take it out on his brother.

Why does Cain do this? Isn't Cain angry with God?

This is a psychological phenomenon known as displaced aggression. When someone experiences anger but feels unable (or unwilling) to express it toward the actual source, they will often redirect that anger towards a safer, more accessible target. Typically this is a spouse, child, sibling or coworker.

In my sibling rivalry with Chuck, my annoyance and anger towards him was really displaced aggression. My true anger was toward my father's rejection and even toward myself due to my inability to please him no matter how hard I tried. But I could not safely express that anger to my father, so I vented it sideways onto my brother.

In this biblical story, and in our lives, it is not the pain or hurt that is experienced, but rather what we choose to do with it that matters most. God knows this. We can release the pain, or we can hold onto it, and thereby open the door for all sorts of dysfunction to enter.

May I ask, what is the deepest pain you have ever experienced? Who has hurt you more than anyone else?

Was it a parent, spouse, child, boss, co-worker, coach, or teacher? Was it someone you trusted?

I want you to revisit that pain and ask yourself – what did you do with the secondary emotions that accompanied it? Is it still affecting you? Have you created a weapon out of your pain that causes you to shut down, lash out, become defensive, or simply detach from people and situations when you are reminded of it? Or have you navigated through that pain, learned the lessons you needed to learn and moved on?

With my brother, once I was out of the house, that dark cloud of anger lifted and I began to know Chuck in ways I'd never seen before. Over the years we have grown closer. Today, Chuck is one of my best friends. He is the most selfless person I know. Gentle, loving, kind and patient, he is an amazing father and husband. While I appreciate the friendship I share with him today, I regret allowing my displaced aggression to blind me as a youngster – I could have used a friend like him back then. When we live from our pain, it blinds us to reality. We see what we want to see – we see what feeds our pain.

With my father, I came to realize that he did the best he could with the example he was given. He was raised by an alcoholic father who was physically abusive. His father, at one point, forced he and his siblings to watch as he held their mother by her hair and beat her with an extension cord. I cannot imagine the long term emotional and psychological damage that was done to them by this. My father was a human. He made mistakes, sure. I have come to believe that despite his shortcomings, his intentions were to be a better father than what he had. He was – and for that I am grateful. There was a time I took the hurt I experienced at his hand, turned it into a weapon and hurt others. Some time back I was able to lay that down, release my father from responsibility and release myself from the prison of resentment.

What is typically happening when anger (in all its forms) crops up in your life? Are there certain situations, relationships or activities that seem to bring out the worst in you? Have you weaponized past hurts, routinely inflicting damage on yourself and those you love?

Why are you angry?

Resentment is often the X that marks the spot for hurt that you have turned into a weapon. Take some time today to reflect and examine your heart for any resentments you have, and see if you can uncover the root. Then release it.

Let them go from what they owe.

It really is that simple. Release your need to extract vengeance from your pain and thereby release yourself. In so doing, you will be fostering empathy, compassion and humility that will produce patience, wisdom and emotional resilience. This will create the space for genuine healing.

And we *all* need that.

CHAPTER THREE

ĻAUGHING OUT ĻOUD

"IS ANYTHING TOO HARD FOR THE LORD?" GENESIS 18:14

H as there ever been a movie that you have seen so often you can quote nearly every line verbatim?

That movie for me is *Top Gun*. I first saw it in the theater when I was 12 in the summer of 1986. Tom Cruise played the lead character, Pete "Maverick" Mitchell. Maverick lives up to his callsign—he's a bold, boundary-pushing pilot whose raw talent is matched only by his disregard for protocol. He thrives on adrenaline, takes risks that others won't, and often bends the rules to achieve results. His flying is exceptional, but his behavior is unpredictable. We find out Maverick isn't just chasing speed – he's chasing his father's shadow, desperate to prove himself. His desire to be great is entangled with a longing for identity, legacy, approval, and his struggle to separate his own worth from his father's story. *This* was a story I identified with. But aside from my emotional connection to Maverick, I loved the flying scenes. The intense dogfighting and the idea of pushing the edge of the envelope in the F-14 "tomcat" thrilled me. Even today, after literally hundreds of times, I do not tire of watching that movie.

However, my fascination with flying and airplanes didn't begin with Top Gun. My father travelled a lot for work, and we would take him to the airport frequently. This was back when anyone could accompany a traveler all the way to the gate. Actually, you didn't even have to be accompanying anyone – whoever wanted to could park, go inside, and go all the way to the gate. You needed a ticket to get on the plane, but the rest of the airport was fair game. I used to ask my mom to take me to the airport so I could sit and watch the airliners taxi, take off, and land. I loved the sounds of their engines as they roared and the odor of the jet exhaust. I was fascinated that something as big and heavy as a fully loaded 737 could actually fly in the air.

A year before Top Gun hit theaters, I first discovered a different kind of pilot hero: Chuck Yeager. Over Christmas break in 1985, I devoured his autobiography, *Yaeger*. What stuck with me wasn't just his combat record, but when he accomplished something everyone said couldn't be done. On October 14th, 1947, Yaeger piloted his plane, the "Glamorous Glennis", past the sound barrier, a feat not previously believed to be possible.

Before Yeager's flight, the term "sound barrier" was not just a metaphor. It was widely regarded as a real, physical limit. It was believed that to attempt to fly an aircraft faster than the speed of sound would be an effort that no aircraft or human could survive. Lord Cherwell (UK scientist and advisor to Churchill) said in the early 1940s: "Supersonic flight is a myth. It violates fundamental laws of aerodynamics." Sir Richard Glazebrook, President of the Royal Aeronautical Society, stated in the 1930s: "It is impossible for man to travel faster than sound."

Breaking the sound barrier stands as a quintessential example of something considered not just dangerous, but inherently impossible – until it wasn't. Trans-Atlantic flight, running a four-minute mile, climbing Mount Everest, walking on the moon... history shows that many "impossible" feats that were met first with laughter, ridicule, or disbelief were eventually proven possible.

"First they ignore you, then they laugh at you, then they fight you, then you win." – *Unknown*

The pattern is familiar: people laugh at what they believe to be impossible. They scoff at the suggestion that something could defy nature, reason, or experience. Sometimes the laughter comes from scientists and engineers. Sometimes from skeptics and critics. But sometimes, it comes from people like you and me when hope feels too far gone, and we've quietly settled into disbelief.

Long before anyone broke the sound barrier or crested Mount Everest, a woman named Sarah laughed at something even more unthinkable: the idea that she would bear a child at ninety. After a lifetime of disappointment, laughter wasn't joy – it was resignation. And yet, as we will see, the God who created natural limitations has never been bound by them.

❋

When we first meet Sarah in the Bible, she's called Sarai – the wife of Abram.

> "And Abram and Nahor took wives. The name of Abram's wife was Sarai, and the name of Nahor's wife, Milcah, the daughter of Haran the father of Mileah and Iscah." Genesis 11:29

In a book (the bible) that, at times, seems to be obsessed with detailed genealogies, we have one of the most significant characters in the overall biblical narrative that is introduced *without one.* Sarai is the wife of Abram. You know, the one who would one day be called Abraham? The founding patriarch of the Jewish people? And while we are told at least a little about Milcah's paternity, Sarai's is conspicuously absent. Why is that?

The first words Scripture uses to describe her come one verse later:

"Now Sarai was barren; she had no child." Genesis 11:30

No story. No background. Just barren.

The word for barren is the Hebrew *'aqar*, which means sterile. Not that she just didn't have children; she was *unable* to bear them.

Before we learn anything else about her – her beauty, her character, her journey – we are told *what she lacks.* That single sentence carries the weight of years. In a culture where a woman's value was often tied to childbearing, Sarai's childlessness wasn't just personal grief – it was public shame. Month after month. Year after year. The ache of waiting gave way to the ache of wondering.

She followed Abram as he followed a God who promised land, descendants, and blessing. But for Sarai, the years only brought more dust, more tents, and no child. It's not hard to imagine how hope turned brittle.

Then, in Genesis 17, something unexpected happens: God changes their names.

"When Abram was ninety-nine years old the LORD appeared to Abram and said to him, "I am God Almighty;

walk before me, and be blameless, that I may make my covenant between me and you, and may multiply you greatly." Then Abram fell on his face. And God said to him, "Behold, my covenant is with you, and you shall be the father of a multitude of nations. No longer shall your name be called Abram, but your name shall be Abraham, for I have made you the father of a multitude of nations." Genesis 17:1-5

"And God said to Abraham, 'As for Sarai your wife, you shall not call her name Sarai, but Sarah shall be her name. I will bless her, and moreover, I will give you a son by her. I will bless her, and she shall become nations; kings of peoples shall come from her.' Then Abraham fell on his face and laughed... and said to himself... 'Shall Sarah, who is ninety years old, bear a child?'" Genesis 17:15-17

Abram becomes Abraham, which means "father of a multitude." And Sarai ("my princess") becomes Sarah – "princess of nations." Names fit for a patriarch and a matriarch. This leaves Abraham literally rolling on the floor laughing. Sarah is 90 years old. Abraham is 99. The idea of new beginnings must have felt absurd.

Some time later, in Genesis 18, the Lord visits again.

"The LORD said, 'I will surely return to you about this time next year, and Sarah your wife shall have a son.' And Sarah was listening at the tent door behind him. Now

Abraham and Sarah were old, advanced in years. The way
of women had ceased to be with Sarah." Genesis 18:10-11

God reiterates the promise that brought laughter from Abraham earlier, and now Sarah overhears the same message. Part of the parenthetical
interlude tells us that they were "old, advanced in years". The text isn't
satisfied telling us they are *zaqen* (translated as "old" and literally means
"ancient") but doubles down on that by saying they are *ba'im bayamim*
(meaning "have come along in days"). As if that is not enough, the bible
then further clarifies by telling us "the way of women had ceased to be
with Sarah." That is *very* polite English. The literal translation is "Sarah
was a well-trodden road."

So when God declares that she will bear a son within the year, Sarah
does what many of us would do:

"So Sarah laughed to herself, saying, 'After I am worn out,
and my lord is old, shall I have pleasure?'" (Gen. 18:12)

This isn't the laughter of joyful surprise. It's the laugh of a lifetime
of disappointment – a sound that leaks out when the heart no longer
knows how to hope.

But God hears that kind of laughter. And He answers it with a question:

"Is anything too hard for the LORD?" (Gen. 18:14)

One year later, that laugh of disbelief turned into a different kind of
laughter altogether.

"The LORD visited Sarah as he had said, and the LORD
did to Sarah as he had promised. And Sarah conceived and
bore Abraham a son in his old age at the time of which
God had spoken to him." (Gen. 21:1–2)

Her son's name was Isaac, which means "he laughs."

The very sound that once echoed with doubt now echoed with joy.
God took Sarah's skeptical chuckle and transformed it into a song of
celebration. Her weary, aged body had not disqualified her. Her years of
disappointment had not dissuaded Him. The timing may have seemed
absurd to her, but it was right on schedule for God.

❋

When I was five years old and we would return from church on
Sunday about noon, my personal Sunday service was just beginning.
Having gotten a good warm-up at the Baptist Church up the street from
our home, I came home and held my own service. My father had made a
wooden chair for me when I was younger that had a seat about the height
of a high-chair that you would put a baby in to sit at a dinner table. Since
I had grown substantially by 5, it was the perfect height to serve as my
pulpit. I took a couple of my football participation ribbons and draped
them over the front of the chair, stood behind it with my opened bible,
and began to preach to my Sunday faithful. My congregation consisted
of my mother. That's it. She was a regular, but I wouldn't say she was
there every Sunday. And definitely not a tither. Nonetheless, even at
that age I felt a strange connection to the bible and to the idea of teaching
it.

At 9 years old, I walked down the aisle to "become a Christian". I used quotes there because my motivation was most definitely not to become a Christian.

A week prior to me walking down the aisle, another long and dry sermon had just wound down. I was sitting in the pew next to my brother Chuck. When we stood to sing "Just as I Am" for the invitation, my mind was well ahead, daydreaming about what I would eat for lunch and about playing football in the front yard afterward. Suddenly, Chuck slipped out into the aisle and began walking forward. What in the world was he doing? I had never been paying attention enough during this part of the service to even know what this part of the service was for. I looked up at my mom, who was wearing an ear-to-ear smile that I had never before seen on her face. Turns out Chuck accepted Jesus into his heart that day. I had no clue what that meant, but what I did understand is what happened when we got home. My mom told my dad (who only went to church with the family on Easter and Christmas). He was so excited that he told Chuck he would buy him anything he wanted.

Say what?

My father was notoriously cheap. For example, one day when I was older he visited a car dealership for an entire week haggling with the salesman over a few dollars. Eventually, he won out. I recall the salesman calling the house to tell him they agreed to his price. They had to call the house because my dad had walked out in dramatic fashion during negotiations for the third day in a row. You would have thought he was brokering peace in the Middle East. I answered the phone when the salesman called. Before handing the phone to my dad, the salesman said, "Hey kid - you know what - your dad is so tight he squeaks when he walks." Later, I told my dad he said that and he beamed with pride.

Now, King Scrooge was suddenly willing to give a blank check to my brother? Chuck quickly piped up that there was something he really wanted and had his eye on... *a watch*. You read that correctly. Again, this was the enigma that was my brother. He must've been the only 10 1/2 year old kid on the planet that when told he could get whatever he wanted, responded with "a watch." Whatever. I didn't have time to worry about him, I had to figure out how I could get in on some of this action.

The following Sunday, I saw the light and walked down the aisle myself. Everyone was so happy I had put Jesus in my heart, but what I really wanted was to put a video game in my hand. I had wanted Space Invaders for our Atari 2600 since last Christmas (when I didn't get it.) As soon as all of the fanfare was over at the church, we went home to tell my dad of my "decision for Christ." Instead of excitement, he looked at me with twinkling skepticism in his eye. "Is that so?" he asked. "Yessir!" I said, "...and since you took Chuck to get whatever he wanted, I'd like to go get Space Invaders." My eagerness surely had revealed my deception to my father – a former cop. Suddenly, I felt dirty all over, and my cheeks flushed. Something inside me pushed to recant and beg for forgiveness, but I knew my father well by this point. Better to hold the line, come what may, than reverse course and reveal myself to be the imposter I was. One thing I knew my father respected was that once you decided to do something, you did it the whole way. No backing out.

He knew what I was up to, I was sure of it, yet said nothing and didn't challenge me. He directed my mom to take me to the store and buy me the video game – he didn't come. After getting the game I rarely played it. I think the way I obtained it ruined any enjoyment I could have gotten from it.

However, at 17 years old, under the guidance of my youth pastor, Greg, I came into a real, actual relationship with Jesus. I didn't tell anyone, though, because everyone already thought I was a Christian, and in my mind, it would have disappointed a lot of people. If not evidenced by my story, I never really understood what Christianity was about growing up. It seemed like a pretty boring hobby to me, and I could think of *much* better ways to spend a Sunday morning. Yet, somehow, I saw something in Greg that was different. I could see how he lived out his faith, how it impacted his decisions, and how loving, patient, and kind he was. It made me want what he had. I prayed a prayer that sounded something like "God, I believe that you are real. I believe you can change people. I see how you lead Greg, and I want that too. I believe Jesus lived and died for me and all my messiness so I could become more like you. Help me to believe more fully. Please come into my life. Amen." I can't explain it even today, but something was born in me that day. A force seemed to come alive inside. Something that was outside of me, yet within. A voice that was not me, but was a part of me now.

About 8 months later, during a presentation that some missionaries were giving at a Sunday evening church service, I felt that voice call to me. As the missionaries asked for volunteers to serve in Korea with them over the summer, I knew it was something I had to do. That 3-month experience was unlike any other I'd had until then or since. I felt that voice inside grow stronger, more personal, more intimate during that time in Korea. As my faith deepened, my enjoyment of the work we did grew each day. Even though we were busy seven days a week and were exhausted at the end of most days, it was fulfilling. When I returned from that trip I felt that voice inside clearly directing me toward full-time vocational ministry. I wasn't sure the context that was supposed to be, but I *was* sure of two things: 1.) I was being called; and 2.) I desperately *did not* want to give my life to ministry.

The next 32 years of my life were a struggle. There were times I ran from that voice and did my best to bury it under a pile of alcohol, promiscuity, and materialism. There were other times I moved toward that voice engaging in church, leading small groups and teaching occasionally. Each time I moved toward it, the voice only got stronger and I would experience feelings of guilt, knowing I wasn't doing what God wanted me to do with my life. Yet my own will prevailed. My life, up until only a few years ago was a wild ride. I have been a cop and put people in jail, and have been to jail myself. I have been a millionaire, and have had a time where I only had $1 left to my name. I have had a job that paid me $600,000 per year, and I have been unemployed. I have had it all, and subsequently lost it all. I eventually reached a point where my list of regrets was longer than my list of accomplishments. I had lived a life dedicated to myself, and at 48 I looked back on the swath of damage left in my wake and wondered what it could have been. But now, it seemed too late. The best of my life was behind me. So it seemed.

It was then that I began to hear that voice again. Not that it had ever left me; it hadn't. It was just that I was listening again. Willing to give it my full attention once more. Even though I felt like my useful days were past, the voice said, "Give me all of what you have left.. it's *not* over... I can still use you... *it's time to live again.*"

In effect it said, "Is anything too hard for the LORD?"

You are holding part of the answer to that question in your hands.

❋

Sarah's story reminds us that when God makes a promise, He is not limited by biology, statistics, or human opinion. He is not restrained by clocks or calendars. He fulfills His word when He chooses to act, not when we've finally worked up enough faith.

Some of us are still waiting for something to be born. A dream, a calling, a relationship, a breakthrough. We may feel like it's too late. Too broken. Too far gone. We smile politely when people say God is faithful – but deep down, we've stopped expecting Him to show up.

Maybe we wouldn't say it out loud, but like Sarah, we've laughed to ourselves. We've stopped praying the bold prayers. We've made peace with the silence.

But the question still stands:

"Is anything too hard for the LORD?"

What seems impossible to us is not difficult for God. What has felt like a delay may be divine preparation. And even when our faith grows tired, He remains faithful.

Just like He did for Sarah, God can still take our skeptical laughter and turn it into Isaac – into joy. Into proof that nothing is too hard for Him.

I still remember sitting in the airport terminal as a kid, watching those jets roar down the runway and lift into the sky. I never stopped being amazed that something so heavy could fly. But now I realize—it wasn't just the aircraft I was fascinated by. It was the idea that something seemingly impossible could actually happen right in front of me.

That's the God we follow. He doesn't just operate in the realm of what's reasonable. He works in the quiet places where hope has worn thin and faith has grown tired.

Sarah's story reminds us that even when we've given up, God hasn't. He is not threatened by our laughter, nor silenced by our doubts. He enters our barrenness – our waiting, our longing, our weariness – and asks us the same question He asked her:

"Is anything too hard for the LORD?"

Maybe your answer today is honest: "Yes, it feels that way."

If that's where you are, you're not alone. Sarah was there too. So was Abraham. So were generations of believers who waited, doubted, and wrestled to believe again. I've been there.

But here's what they discovered—and what we can, too:

When God speaks, even laughter can become prophecy.

And what once made us laugh in disbelief may one day make us laugh in wonder.

Is anything too hard for the LORD?

Chapter Four

WHEREVER YOU GO... THERE YOU ARE

"AND BEHOLD, THERE CAME A VOICE TO HIM AND SAID 'WHAT ARE YOU DOING HERE ELIJAH?'" 1 KINGS 19:3

From the earliest ages I can remember until I was about 12 years old, it was a family tradition most evenings to sit around the TV from 6-8pm and watch our favorite shows. Some of our favorites were Gilligan's Island, The Love Boat, Happy Days, and my personal favorite – CHiPs. CHiPs was a show about two California Highway Patrol motorcycle officers – Jon Baker and Frank Poncherello (known as "Ponch"). It was a light-hearted police drama about events that occurred as these two patrolled the freeways of Los Angeles. Jon was the steady, responsible one, and Ponch was charismatic, impulsive, and occasionally bent the rules. The Yin and Yang of Southern California law enforcement. I idolized the two characters. For Christmas one year, Chuck and I both got a CHiPs pretend costume set that came with a gold and blue helmet, gun belt (with gun), police baton, handcuffs, and a badge. All plastic, of course. That Christmas afternoon, we took the discarded cardboard containers that were in the garage from our dad's cases of beer and fashioned them into a type of "fairing" for our bicycles. We drew and colored blue and red circles on the cardboard and taped them to the front of our handlebars. After donning our equipment and badges, we patrolled our neighborhood on our bikes, pretending to be Ponch and John.

I knew then that as soon as I was old enough, I would become a police officer.

I still recall my first day at the police academy in San Angelo, Texas, when I was just 20 years old. I wasn't even old enough to buy my own gun. It was a running joke around the academy that I had to train with "daddy's pistol", which was true – my dad had to buy it for me. Nevertheless, I was determined to be tops in my class. I dove into the Penal Code and the Texas Code of Criminal Procedure like it was the Bible. I spent my evenings in my furnished efficiency apartment eating "heat and serve" microwave dinners, studying and highlighting the ins and outs of the law. When I stood for graduation, I took the oath and still remember having my badge pinned on my uniform. My heart was beating so hard, I could feel the heavy metal rising then dropping with a thud on my chest with each beat. I went to the bathroom, and when I looked in the mirror, I just stood there for a few seconds. My eyes took it all in - the deep navy blue, nearly black uniform that was pressed and creased; the lapel pins and patches on the shoulders; the badge; my belt with the attached handcuffs, ASP baton, pepper spray, additional magazines full of bullets, and that gun. Feeling the weight of all of the equipment and its attendant responsibility that had just been conferred on me was overwhelming. Me – still a relative kid – now had been charged with the responsibility of serving and protecting the citizens of San Angelo– up to and including giving my life if necessary; I was also given the power to take away someone's immediate freedom via arrest – to even take their life if necessary. It was a surreal moment looking at myself in that mirror. I was a police officer. It was one of the proudest moments of my life.

As a police officer, like most jobs, many of your friends wind up being the people that you work with. Mostly, it was those officers you were on the same shift with. For instance, while I knew officers who were on the other shifts, I rarely saw them, and we lived different hours. Police work being a 24-hour-a-day operation, often other officers were sleeping when I was working and vice versa. However, there were times when I would meet some guys who weren't on my shift, and for whatever reason, we hit it off. One of those guys was Jaime Padron. Jaime joined the PD a year after I did. Jaime was a former Marine and was what you might think of when you think of a Marine – muscular, thick, direct, disciplined, loyal, and aggressive – all with a flat-top haircut. Jaime and I really clicked – I'm not even fully sure why to this day. We had the same days off (Mon, Tues and Wed), even though he worked the swing shift (4pm – 2am) and I worked deep nights (9pm – 7am), we started to hang out on our days off. There were weeks when we would spend our entire time off together. Typically beginning with lunch at "Mejor Que Nada" – a Mexican restaurant whose name translates to "better than nothing". We would sit at the bar and load up on chips, salsa, enchiladas and three or four Modelo beers. After that, if either of us had errands to run, we would frequently accomplish those things together. No matter what we needed to do in the afternoon, by 6pm you could usually find us at the "5 point lounge" – somewhat known as a cop bar with a cop-friendly owner and bartenders. By cop-friendly I mean they gave us drink specials. For $2 you could get a Crown and Coke that was about 7/8th's Crown. We'd play pool, darts, flirt with the girls, and engage in deep conversation about our lives, problems, hopes, and dreams. We'd usually close the place down. About 11:30am the next day, you could find us both back at Mejor Que Nada for round two. And so it went.

Because our shifts overlapped, there were many times when Jaime and I would get sent to calls together – some of them quite dangerous. One night when clearing a call, Jaime and I were standing by our cruisers talking, and in the middle of the conversation, I heard a high-pitched "ZZiP.... ZZiP" that sounded like a bee going by my ear at Mach 2. Fractions of a second later, I heard the crack of a gun, and Jaime's shoulder crashed into my torso, tackling me in the grass behind my unit while he yelled "shooter!". As we scrambled to our knees and withdrew our pistols, Jaime pointed south, where an open lot lay, indicating this was the direction from where the shots came. We radioed in to dispatch while shuffling in a low crouch with our weapons pointed ahead, moving towards the lot. The smell of fresh gunpowder hung in the air, but we couldn't find anyone. Ultimately, after searching for about 10 minutes, we left the area and went back to patrol. I guess someone wanted to take a couple of pot shots at the police that night. What I didn't know initially was that the "ZZiP" sound I heard was the sound of the bullets going by. Jaime, having seen action as a Marine in Iraq, knew this. When a supersonic round is fired from a gun, if you are downrange, the bullet will hit its target before you can hear the sound of the gun going off – the bullet is traveling faster than the speed of sound – which is why I heard the zip of the bullet before hearing the report of the gun. There was more than one night Jaime likely saved my life – this being one of them. Nothing on earth will draw you closer to another person than placing your life in their hands. If they don't do their part, you could die. If you don't do your part, they could. It's one reason for the brotherhood of police officers – you just can't know that feeling until you've experienced it. Once experienced, you can never forget it. For all these reasons and many others, I loved Jaime like a brother.

I came of age in San Angelo. I saw things as a police officer that most people never get the chance to see, and some things most people would never want to see. I developed the hard, cynical outer shell most cops wear for the public and a deep respect and love for my fellow brothers in blue. The deepest relationships I've ever had were born in San Angelo, and I haven't been able to replicate them since. If given the chance, I would live those years over and over again. It was the time of my life, and to this day, it is the best job I have ever had.

Unfortunately, after a few years and two kids, I realized I was not earning enough as a police officer to support my family and have any kind of savings. I worried if I would ever be able to retire or help my kids go to college. I decided to leave police work and San Angelo, moving to Dallas to work in financial services. While I still kept in touch with Jaime, over the years the contact became few and far between as he also had moved on to Austin PD, and I was promoted with my company and moved to Illinois.

On April 6, 2012, I was up early reading my bible in our living room at our home in Springfield, Illinois. It also happened to be Good Friday. As I was sitting in the pre-dawn darkness about 5am my cell phone lit up and buzzed on the table next to me. It was an incoming call from Rob Parry – another brother in blue from San Angelo who had become one of my best friends. It was unusual for Rob to call me this early. I don't remember what I said when I answered the phone, but I will never forget his first words - "Jaime is dead. He was killed this morning on duty." I instantly felt dizzy and nauseous. Rob gave me as many details as he knew. Jaime had been dispatched about 2:30am to a shoplifter at a Walmart in north Austin. Upon arrival and making contact with the suspect, the suspect started to run for the exit. Jaime tackled him as they were nearing the front door, and somewhere in the struggle, the suspect produced a gun, shooting twice. One round striking Jaime in the bulletproof vest, and the fatal round striking him in his neck. Jaime passed quickly due to rapid blood loss. Rob promised to keep me updated, and we hung up. I felt a hard, cold loneliness creep over me as I began to sob.

I hadn't been back to San Angelo in the 12 years that had passed since I left. I first went back for Jaime's funeral. Soon after the funeral, I found myself making trips back to San Angelo whenever I was back in Texas. I would go back and visit people who were a significant part of my life when I lived there – people I had lost contact with. I started going back to the 5-point lounge when in town, and other places I would frequent with Jaime. I would go to Jaime's grave site each time and sit on the bench in front of his grave and talk with him, pouring out a Modelo near the headstone and drinking one for myself. On one of these trips I drove around to all of the places Jaime and I had experienced dangerous situations as police officers together. I took pictures of each place on my cell phone, driving all over the northside of town one afternoon to accomplish the task. Back in my hotel room later that evening, I was going through these photos and reliving these moments through tears. It was at this moment I looked out of the window of my hotel, and a question cropped up from somewhere deep inside: Why are you here?

Why was I here? Why, after all these years of having put San Angelo in the rearview mirror, was I now coming back so often? What was I looking for? Then it dawned on me.

While I can return to the physical location... I cannot go back in time. I can come back *here*, but I can't go back *there*. And *there* is what I was really seeking.

◉

"And when Elijah heard it, he wrapped his face in his cloak and went out and stood at the entrance of the cave. And behold, there came a voice to him and said 'What are you doing here Elijah?'" 1 Kings 19:13

The story of Elijah is a wild one, and I will do my best to provide a concise background to set the stage properly.

Elijah is what is referred to as a prophet. A prophet was a person chosen and authorized by God to speak on His behalf. Today we often think of prophets as "seers" declaring future events, but in the bible, more often they were calling people to return to faithful obedience to God. In the 9th century BC, Elijah first appears on the scene in the Old Testament, here in 1 Kings. We are told nothing about his background, except that he is from Tishbe. Tishbe was a small settlement in a rugged wilderness area located east of the Jordan River, and situated in the modern day country of Jordan. Elijah arrives during a significant religious crisis.

After the death of King Solomon (930 BC) the kingdom of Israel split in half. The northern kingdom retained the name "Israel" and the southern kingdom was called "Judah". Samaria was chosen to be the capital of the northern kingdom. The king of the north, Omri, hired Phoenician artisans to construct Samaria as a proper capital, but this was quite expensive. To help offset the costs of the build, Omri's son Ahab entered into an arranged marriage with a Phoenician princess – Jezebel.

Jezebel agreed on one condition: her religion of Baal worship must be established in Israel. Ahab agreed and eventually succeeded his father as king.

Baal, often depicted as a warrior riding the clouds, was the god of storms who sent the life-preserving rain. As the story goes, Baal was locked in a perpetual battle with a god named Mot. Mot was the god of death and drought. This myth helped to explain the annual change in seasons, with Baal's victory over Mot bringing life-giving rain and fertility to the ground. Mot's triumph over Baal would result in drought. However, Mot's victory was always seen as temporary, as Baal is eventually resurrected and brought rain again. Thus were explained the annual changes in the ancient Near Eastern climate.

Baal worship involved ritual sacrifices, sexual immorality and child sacrifice. Ahab built an altar to Baal in Samaria (1 Kings 16:32), and Baal worship became widespread, state-sponsored and deeply integrated into society in the northern kingdom.

Let's pick it up in 1 Kings 17:

> "Now Elijah the Tishbite, of Tisbe in Gilead, said to Ahab, 'As the LORD, the God of Israel, lives, before whom I stand, there shall be neither dew nor rain these years, except by my word." 1 Kings 17:1

Elijah seeks out King Ahab and tells him that it will not rain again until Elijah says so. In fact, there won't even be so much as dew on the ground – zero moisture – until Elijah gives the word. We might read this as simply a punishment directed at King Ahab from God for leading the people astray however, it is also an attack on the god that is attracting the worship of the people, as Baal is the god of rain.

"And the word of the LORD came to him: 'Depart from
here and turn eastward and hide yourself by the brook
Cherith, which is east of the Jordan." 1 Kings 17: 2-5

God tells Elijah to go hide, and he does. For three years. THREE
years. No rain; no dew. The people expected to be without rain for
a season, and surely a year-long drought wasn't unheard of, but not a
drop of rain for *three years*? Where was their god Baal? Unlike the
confrontation between Baal and Mot, Baal is nowhere to be found in
this confrontation with the Lord and, as one scholar puts it, is now being
"shown to have no power at all in the realm that is supposed to be his –
the sending of the annual rains. He is, in fact, quite dead." [1]

"After many days the word of the LORD came to Elijah,
in the third year, saying 'Go show yourself to Ahab, and
I will send rain upon the earth.' So Elijah went to show
himself to Ahab. Now the famine was severe in Samaria."
1 Kings 18:1-2

God tells Elijah to come out of hiding and to find Ahab. This
three-year absence of moisture has led to severe famine. With an economy built on the back of agriculture, this would have been devastating.
Consider that here in the United States, economic conditions leading up
to an election play a significant factor in who is ultimately elected pres-

---

1. Hauser, Alan J., and Gregory, Russell, eds. *From Carmel to Horeb :
Elijah in Crisis*. London: Bloomsbury Publishing Plc, 1990.

ident. James Carville, political pundit and lead strategist for Bill Clinton's successful 1992 presidential campaign, famously wrote on a sign in the campaign's Little Rock, Arkansas headquarters: "It's the economy, stupid." This was to remind staff that the key issue that mattered most was the struggling U.S. economy.

In modern times, when you are the Chief Executive and the economy struggles, you may lose your office. In the ancient Near East, you may lose your head. King Ahab was under significant pressure.

> "When Ahab saw Elijah, Ahab said to him, 'Is it you, you troubler of Israel?' And he answered, 'I have not troubled Israel, but you have, and your father's house, because you have abandoned the commandments of the LORD and followed the Baals. Now therefore send and gather all Israel to me at Mount Carmel, and the 450 prophets of Baal and the 400 prophets of Asherah, who eat at Jezebel's table.'" 1 Kings 18:17-19

We get a glimpse of just how out of hand worship of Baal has become, as there are 450 prophets of Baal, and Israel's worship of other gods has spread beyond Baal worship – also mentioned is an additional 400 prophets of Asherah. Asherah was a Canaanite goddess who was associated with fertility, sexuality and motherhood. To say that Israel has strayed from the LORD is a dramatic understatement.

Elijah sets up a showdown on the top of Mount Carmel – the invitees are King Ahab, all of the prophets of Baal and Asherah, and all of the people of the northern kingdom.

"So Ahab sent to all the people of Israel and gathered the prophets together at Mount Carmel. And Elijah came near to all the people and said, 'How long will you go limping between two different opinions? If the LORD is God, follow him; but if Baal, then follow him.' And the people did not answer him a word." 1 Kings 18:21

As previously mentioned, a prophet's job was primarily to draw the people back to faithful worship of the Lord. As such, Elijah is said to have addressed the people – he is not talking to the prophets or Baal or Asherah or Ahab – at least not yet. Elijah makes it clear that the people have to choose – they cannot continue to "limp" between the LORD and Baal.

The people's response? They "did not answer him a word." Silence.

Elijah suggests a contest. He recommends that the prophets of Baal be given a bull to sacrifice to their god, and that he also be given a bull to sacrifice to the Lord. Each will build an altar, cut the bull into pieces, and lay it on the wood of their altar. The only condition is that no fire would be applied to the sacrifice by the prophets – that would be supplied by the respective deity as evidence of their existence.

"And you will call upon the name of your god, and I will call upon the name of the LORD, and the God who answers by fire, he is God." 1 Kings 18:24

The people agreed that this made good sense, and the prophets of Baal went first. The text tells us that they prepared the sacrifice, placed it on their altar, and "called upon the name of Baal from morning until noon,

saying, 'O Baal, answer us!' But there was no voice, and no one answered."
I Kings 18:26

At this point, Elijah begins to mock them, essentially saying, "You guys should cry louder! He is probably just daydreaming... or going to the bathroom. He could be on a long trip, or maybe just asleep. You guys are going to have to wake him up!" (1 Kings 18:27)

> "And they cried aloud and cut themselves after their cus-
> tom with swords and lances, until the blood gushed out
> upon them. And as midday passed, they raved on until
> the time of the offering of the oblation, but there was no
> voice. No one answered; no one paid attention." 1 Kings
> 18:28-29

If nothing else, these folks are serious. Dedicated. Sincere. Desperate. *Cutting themselves.* However, sincerity is not the test for truth. A person can be sincere and still be sincerely wrong.

Elijah then calls all of the people close, and the text says that he repaired the altar of the LORD that "had been thrown down". It had long been discarded as the worship of Baal took over. Elijah takes 12 stones and rebuilds the altar and makes a circular trench in the ground all the way around it. He then cuts his bull into pieces and lays it on the altar. Elijah tells the people to pour water on the sacrifice and the wood until it is not only soaked but until it fills up the trench he has cut around the altar. He is stacking the deck against the LORD.

Elijah prays aloud to the LORD.

> "Then the fire of the LORD fell and consumed the burnt
> offering and the wood and the stones and the dust, and

licked up the water that was in the trench. And when all
the people saw it, they fell on their faces and said, 'The
LORD, he is God; the LORD, he is God." And Elijah said
to them, 'Seize the prophets of Baal, let not one of them
escape.' And they seized them. And Elijah brought them
down to the brook Kishon and slaughtered them there."
1 Kings 18:38-40

Not only that, but:

"And in a little while the heavens grew black with clouds
and wind, and there was a great rain. And Ahab rode
and went to Jezreel. And the hand of the LORD was
on Elijah, and he gathered up his garment and ran before
Ahab to the entrance of Jezreel." 1 Kings 18:45-46

Let's pause now and soak in this great victory Elijah must have been
sensing. He has been in hiding for three years, and the drought he
commanded at God's word has brought the nation to its knees in severe
famine. All alone, he confronted the *entire kingdom*, which led to a
dramatic showdown between Baal and the LORD. Elijah saw God's
great deliverance and victory unfold right in front of him. Then, with
the help of the people who were indecisive only moments ago, he puts all
of the prophets of Baal to the sword. Now, somehow, he outruns Ahab
(who is in a chariot), and makes it to the entrance of Jezreel before him.

What would *you* have been feeling? Invincible. Unstoppable. Fear-
less.

Why is Ahab going to Jezreel? It was a secondary capital, where he would have had a palace, but also this is apparently where Jezebel is. He is going to tell Jezebel all that has happened.

Why is Elijah going to Jezreel? Remember, as a prophet, Elijah's ultimate goal is a national return to faithful worship of the LORD alone. Don't you imagine that now Elijah is sensing that the entire people will return to the LORD in repentance and end their worship of Baal? That perhaps even King Ahab will issue a decree across the nation for a national day of prayer and a destruction of all things associated with Baal worship? What if Jezebel herself realizes that Baal is no god at all, and devotes herself to the LORD God? Elijah wants a front row seat.

You and I would say – he is *there for it.*

Now that God had shown up in a decisive victory, and is sending the rain the land and people so desperately need... what else could the response possibly be?

> "Ahab told Jezebel all that Elijah had done, and how he
> had killed all the prophets with the sword. Then Jezebel
> sent a messenger to Elijah, saying, 'So may the gods do to
> me and more also if I do not make your life as the life of
> one of them by this time tomorrow." 1 Kings 19:1-2

Instead of repentance, Jezebel issues Elijah's death warrant.

❂

Where do you go when it all falls apart?

I left police work for a job as a financial advisor at Edward Jones. I found the work interesting and challenging. The basic job was obtaining clients. The way of Edward Jones at the time was going door to door and making what was referred to as 25 "real" contacts per day. A "real" contact was someone to whom I spoke, obtained their contact information, and pitched an investment. While it felt like each day was a long slog of pride-swallowing, door slammed in your face, running from dogs death march... by the time I was a year in I had an office in Grapevine and had an assistant. While things were going well, my business was not prepared to sustain the shockwave of the 9/11 attacks. As the markets plunged, most of my clients moved their investments to cash, or withdrew their them altogether. Frankly, I didn't blame them. What was happening seemed unprecedented, and I lacked the experience to know how to properly advise them. My business and income tanked.

While I knew my performance was not up to company standards, I was not expecting the call I got the day before Thanksgiving in 2001. My area leader called and in an emotionless tone essentially told me that I had one month to revive my business or I would be terminated. In lieu of termination, I could resign. In my view there was really no choice, as a termination on a U-4 would make it more difficult to get hired in the industry.

I "resigned". It was effective immediately.

At the time, I had a wife and a set of two-year-old twins at home. When I hung up the phone, my thoughts immediately turned to them and my stomach went into free-fall. How was I going to provide for them? How were we going to make rent? What will my wife say? My in-laws? I sat at my desk, stunned for what was surely only a few minutes but felt like hours.

I exited my office, sent my assistant home for the day, then locked the door, sat at her desk, and cried.

A new career that seemingly started so well and was on the right trajectory changed in one day in September. I wanted to go home. Not my home in town, but my parents' house. I wanted to get away from here – away from this job, away from this city. Go get one of my mom's hugs. Have her pray for me. Have her tell me it was going to be ok. Even though I had challenges with my father growing up, whenever I went back home, I always felt like I was walking into a shelter; as if the outside world couldn't hurt me here. I knew if I had nothing else, I always had home.

That's exactly what we did. I left work, went to my house, and announced we were going to my parents for Thanksgiving. I called my dad and cleared the trip with him, though I knew he'd say yes. We packed our kids and clothes in the car and drove the four hours it took to get from DFW to Lawton, Ok. As soon as I turned down their long gravel driveway, I began to feel better already.

●

Jezebel sends a messenger to tell Elijah: "You are a dead man." Elijah's response?

"Then he was afraid, and he arose and ran for his life..." 1
Kings 19:4

Those same feet that carried Elijah the 17 miles from Mount Carmel to Jezreel in jubilant victory, make an about-face and start heading for the hills out of a desire to preserve his life.

"...and (Elijah) came to Beersheba, which belongs to Judah, and left his servant there. But he himself went a day's

journey into the wilderness and came and sat down under
a broom tree. And he asked that he might die, saying, 'It
is enough; now, O LORD, take away my life, for I am no
better than my fathers.'" I Kings 19: 3b-4

Elijah flees south and makes it into the southern kingdom (remember
the nation had split in two), where Jezebel had no authority. Even
though he is now reasonably safe, we see that this must not have been
the only thing he was seeking, because after telling his servant to stay
behind, he "went a day's journey into the wilderness" and sat down under
a broom tree. Having been to Israel and seen many broom trees, I would
be hesitant to call it a "tree" as we know it. It is more like a glorified
bush. However, it is one of the few places a person can find shade in the
Israeli desert wilderness. This is a sad sight – after this great victory Elijah
participates in on Mount Carmel, a mere day or two later, he is fleeing for
his life, alone in a desert, and seeking shelter by crawling under a bush. If
the mental image doesn't inspire sympathy, then surely his request does:
"O LORD, take away my life, for I am no better than my fathers."

"God, kill me." This seems extreme until you consider how Elijah has
spent the last three years working alongside God according to His plan,
has not only seen the miraculous along the way, but has also been the
instrument God used to complete many miracles. Then, in complete
obedience to God, he confronts an entire nation with its civic and religious leaders standing by, and orchestrates one of the most dramatic
miracles history has ever known. What would you think after all that?
Wouldn't you think – finally! It's all coming together! We are going to
return as a nation, en masse, to the pure worship of the one true God,
and He is doing it through me!

This was something all of the prophets before him desired to do but were not able to accomplish – and Elijah is seeing it happen. Or so he thought. I imagine the last thing that he expected to happen when he got to Jezreel is for Jezebel to put a contract out on him. Elijah is confused, confounded, and cuts out... knowing that Jezebel has the means and the authority to complete her threat.

So he sets out into the southern desert, lies down under a shrub, and asks God to take his life. What is the reasoning he gives? "For I am no better than my fathers..." This implies that Elijah expected to be. Again, all the prophets before him had not seen the level of success Elijah had in their proclamations. Yet now they were coming for his life, just as they had the prophets before him. It has all fallen apart. All of his expectations, all of his hopes... all of that work he put in. For what? Has his life made any real impact? Why did you have me do all that, God? Was it ever really your voice I was hearing in the first place?

I have never been suicidal, but I've had a few low times in my life when things came to pieces, confusion reigned, and despair set in. Times when I prayed "God, if I don't wake up tomorrow... I'd be ok with that." I think this is what Elijah was feeling.

Elijah falls asleep under that bush, and twice we are told an Angel of the LORD appeared to him, providing him bread and water, then says to him:

"Arise and eat, for the journey is too great for you." 1Kings 19:7

What journey? Clearly, Elijah has a destination in mind that is beyond this shrub he is lying under, and the angel knows it. Wherever he is headed, there isn't enough fuel in the tank to get him all the way there, so he needs a fill-up.

> "And he arose and ate and drank, and went in the strength of that food forty days and forty nights to Horeb, the mount of God." 1 Kings 19:8

Elijah has been headed to Horeb since he beat feet out of Jezreel. It's quite a journey – 40 days to get there. In scripture, the number 40 often represents times of trial and testing. The earth was flooded by 40 days and nights of rain, the Israelites wandered in the desert for 40 years, and Jesus is in the wilderness for 40 days fasting and being tempted. There are other examples, I am just making the point that by using the number 40, we are being told Elijah is going through a time of trial, testing, and deep introspection.

Why is he going to Horeb, and why is it referred to as "the mount of God"? Mount Horeb has a long and storied history in the Old Testament, but it is not always referred to as "Horeb". It is also known by another name – Mount Sinai.

Mount Sinai is where Moses first encounters God in the burning bush (Exodus 3:1), God descends on the mountain in the sight of the nation of Israel (Exodus 19), and God appears before Moses on Mount Sinai (Exodus 33, 34). This mountain was the historical location of a divine encounter where God revealed Himself in profound ways.

Elijah is going "home", so to speak. Back to a place where hearing from God was obvious and his instructions were clear. When contact with Him was as simple as heading up the mountain. When obedience was easier, and the costs weren't as high. He has been obedient to God in every way He has asked, it still became a dumpster fire, and now Elijah wants answers and maybe a little bit of comfort.

> "There he came to a cave and lodged in it. And behold, the word of the LORD came to him, and he said to him, 'What are you doing here, Elijah?'" 1 Kings 19:9

The question in Hebrew is "Mah leka poh, Elijah?" Literally translated, "What is for you here, Elijah?" God is not simply asking Elijah why is he in the physical location that he is in. God is asking him, "What exactly are you hoping to find here, Elijah?"

The implication is that whatever Elijah is looking for, isn't found here – at least not anymore.

Because while Elijah can come back *here*... he can't go back *there*.

❦

That Thanksgiving at my parents' house after I resigned my job was a nice retreat from "the real world". However, it was not permanent. I shared with my parents the reason for our last-minute trip and my desire to get out of dodge for a couple of days. My parents appreciated the sentiment, but also had some direct advice. "You can lick your wounds for a couple of days, but all the issues you faced driving up here are still waiting for you back in DFW. The sooner you get to addressing them, the better", my dad said. My mom hugged me and said, "I wish I could make it all go away – but you are a big boy now. You will get through this."

The days of having everything corrected when I went back home were over. Sure, I had their support, and it was nice to feel it; but the important work lie ahead.

"Mah leka poh, Elijah?" What is for you... here?

> "He (Elijah) said, "I have been very jealous for the LORD,
> the God of hosts. For the people of Israel have forsaken
> your covenant, thrown down your altars, and killed your
> prophets with the sword, and I, even I only, am left, and
> they seek my life, to take it away.'" 1 Kings 19:14

Translation: "I've done everything that you have asked me to do, and
not only have the people not returned to you, but anyone who was on
my side is now dead, I am the only one left and they are trying to kill
me." Listen to Elijah's words.... "*I* have been very jealous... and *I*... even *I*
only, am left..." and who has Elijah been working for all by himself? "*Your*
covenant... *your* altars... *your* prophets..." Almost as if to say – "So what
are you going to do about it?"

God is direct with Elijah:

> "Go, return on your way to the wilderness of Damascus.
> And when you arrive, you shall anoint Hazael to be king
> over Syria. And Jehu the son of Nimshi you shall anoint
> to be king over Israel, and Elisha the son of Shaphat of
> Abel-meholah you shall anoint to be prophet in your
> place." 1 Kings 19:15-16

Elijah makes a long journey for a short conversation. After asking
Elijah, "What are you doing here?", which has the additional implication
of "you shouldn't be here", God tells him to turn around and go back
where he came from, gives him specific directions on who to anoint as

leaders, and makes a plan to replace Elijah. "My will for you is not here, Elijah... my will for you is heading back into the mess that you ran from."

Elijah's future was not in looking toward the past for direction; it was in returning to what he was running from.

You can't drive a car forward by looking in the rearview mirror.

※

In my hotel room that night in San Angelo, I thought about my time as a police officer in that town. It was the first time in my life that I felt I had an impact. I could look myself in the mirror at the end of a shift and know that my life had mattered that day – that I did something worth doing. My confidence in who I was as a person was strong. I enjoyed some of the best friendships and relationships I've ever had. My days working were filled with significance, my days off were filled with fun and I knew my place in the world. Since leaving San Angelo, somewhere along the way, in my chase for material success, I had lost things that were fundamental to a meaningful life.

After my world had been rocked by Jaime's murder, I realized that I wanted that sense of true north again. That sense I had when I was in my early twenties, patrolling the streets and chasing bad guys with my best friends. However misguided, I kept returning to the place, hoping to recapture the reality.

When things fall apart, we often go back. We break up with a partner and go back to a relationship that wasn't really working, but at least we know what to expect. We tried a new career that didn't work out as planned, and so we went back to what we had always done before.

When a loved one dies, when we lose our job, when we break up or get divorced, move to a new town, suffer a significant moral failure, or experience any other substantial event, it often ushers in a time of uncertainty and fear of the unknown future. In these moments, we often return to things we know are comfortable, even when we know it's not the best thing for our growth going forward. Old relationships, old friends, old habits, old haunts. But if we are constantly going back, we can never actually move forward.

We all suffer setbacks as humans. The danger lies in how we respond. We've suffered a painful loss, and we don't want to feel those feelings again or risk feeling them anymore, so we go back to the place where it's comfortable. A temporary layover in the terminal of comfort is fine. But some of us miss our departing flight and we get stuck there. We stop trying, we stop putting ourselves out there, and we stop moving forward.

We settle into living a timid life, insulating us from defeat, but inoculating us from victory. We were not created to live that way.

Retrieving the question from Chapter 1 – Where are you? Are you stuck?

Have you stopped trying out of fear? Have you suffered some serious losses and are now operating within your comfort zone, afraid to take risks? Do you find yourself yearning for "the good old days" when things seemed easier and you seemed happier?

What are you doing here?

Some of us have quit growing. We've stopped taking risks.

We have pulled off the freeway and put the car in park. No real need to go beyond the point we have reached in life.

That is a problem.

Your soul was created to grow, and grow continually. When things stagnate, they begin to die. That includes you. It is a biological fact that if you are not growing, you are dying.

It is a problem physically, but a more serious problem spiritually.

How would you describe your spiritual life? Vibrant, growing, re-freshing? Or stagnant, bland, and impotent? If you were to take a piece of paper and draw a line illustrating the trajectory in your relationship with God over the last year, what would that line look like? Up and to the right, down and to the left, or mostly flat?

Do you have a hunger for a deeper understanding of God and his ways, or little interest in reading and applying scripture? Is your prayer life rich, life giving and deep, or minimal, mechanical, or simply absent? Do you find yourself prioritizing obedience to God or comfort and entertainment?

Do you see your best spiritual life ahead, or in the rearview mirror?

Is your soul growing, or is your soul dying?

In the first chapter, we tackled the question, "Where are you?" Wherever you find yourself, here is the question:

What are you doing here?

CHAPTER FIVE

THICK AS THIEVES

"HAS THIS HOUSE, WHICH IS CALLED BY MY NAME, BECOME A DEN OF ROBBERS IN YOUR EYES?" JEREMIAH 7:11

Robert LeRoy Parker was born on April 13th, 1866, in Utah. The first of 13 children, Parker grew up learning horsemanship and ranching. Parker left home as a teenager, apprenticing for a short time with a butcher, followed by working on several ranches. On one of those ranches, Parker met a cattle thief and outlaw by the name of Mike Cassidy. Under Cassidy's influence, Parker soon found himself drawn to a life outside the law, rustling cattle and other livestock from rival ranches. Eventually, Parker sank deeper into criminal activity, and on June 24, 1889, he robbed his first bank. After the robbery, Parker began using an alias he developed from a combination of his early years as a butcher and a nod to his mentor in crime, Mike Cassidy. From now on, Robert LeRoy Parker would be known as "Butch Cassidy".

The first bank he robbed, the San Miguel Valley Bank in Telluride, Colorado, was a big score. Cassidy fled with $21,000 in cash (equivalent of more than $700,000 in 2025) to a remote hideout in the southeastern corner of Utah known as "Robbers Roost". Robbers Roost became one of the most infamous outlaw hideouts in the American West. Situated among the remote canyons, the terrain is so difficult that even today, most of it is only accessible on foot or horseback. The Roost offered natural concealment, perfect vantage points to spot anyone approaching, and multiple escape routes. While many outlaws occasionally used the sanctuary of the Roost to hide after committing crimes, Cassidy and his gang – "The Wild Bunch"- used it as a strategic base of operations between criminal episodes of bank heists, train robberies and rustling operations. No lawman is ever known to have successfully penetrated Robbers Roost during its active years as a haven for criminals. It was the perfect place to divide up the loot, rest and recover, plan future scores, and avoid capture.

It was a true "den of robbers."

❁

"Has this house, which is called by my name, become a den of robbers in your eyes?" Jeremiah 7:11

For all the advancements of technology over time, human nature hasn't changed much. Jeremiah uttered these words in about 600 B.C. In those days, after committing a crime, bandits would often seek the concealment and safety of caves in the Judean hills until their pursuers gave up the search. They would then emerge to commit other crimes. A cave used for this purpose was known as a "den of robbers".

The "house" referred to in this verse is the Temple in Jerusalem. More specifically, it is the "Second Temple" as it was built to replace Solomon's Temple (the first one), which was destroyed by the Babylonians in 586 B.C. The temple was the very center of Israel's worship of the one true God, Yahweh. It was the place where teaching and prayer occurred, sacrificial worship was conducted, and pilgrimage feasts were carried out. It housed the Holy Place and the "Holy of Holies", believed to be where God Himself resided, and was only accessible by the High Priest once per year on the Day of Atonement (Yom Kippur).

Jeremiah is a prophet. As you recall, prophets were those given authority to speak on God's behalf – the mouthpiece of God to the people. The question we are considering is a question in a broader message God has told Jeremiah to give the people who are worshipping at the temple.

> "The word that came to Jeremiah from the LORD: 'Stand in the gate of the LORD's house, and proclaim there this word and say, "Hear the word of the LORD, all you men of Judah who enter these gates to worship the LORD. Thus says the LORD of hosts, the God of Israel: 'Amend your ways and your deeds, and I will let you dwell in this place. Do not trust in these deceptive words: "This is the temple of the LORD, the temple of the LORD, the temple of the LORD."'" Jeremiah 7:1-4

When God says, "I will let you dwell in this place", He is referring to the very turbulent political environment. This message is given between the fall of the Assyrian empire and the rise of the Babylonian empire.

What the future possesses, and who might possess *them*, was a serious concern. God is telling them, "if you amend your ways, whoever is the dominant power in the world going forward will not displace you as a people – I will cause them to let you continue to live here." The implication is, of course, if they do not "amend" their ways, then He won't let them live here.

The popular belief at this time was that the temple itself was some sort of good luck charm. It was viewed as a guarantee of the presence and protection of God as a result of the covenant that God had made with David in 2 Samuel 7. That covenant promised that David's kingdom would be established forever. As a result, the people felt untouchable and assured of God's protection. God's word to the people through Jeremiah assures them that *they are wrong*.

> "For if you truly amend your ways and your deeds, if you truly execute justice with one another, if you do not oppress the sojourner, the fatherless, or the widow, or shed innocent blood in this place, and if you do not go after other gods to your own harm, then I will let you dwell in this place, in the land that I gave of old to your fathers forever." Jeremiah 7:5-7

The people are coming to the temple for worship and performing the rituals of the temple while at the same time paying no attention to what God had always demanded ethically. They had no concern for the most vulnerable of society: the widow, the orphan, and the immigrant. On top of this they were running after other gods. As a boss of mine once said, "That dog don't hunt."

"Behold, you trust in deceptive words to no avail." Jeremiah 7:8

God declares that believing that they are safe merely because of the building is "deceptive". The root word in Hebrew is *shehker,* and also means "fraudulent" when used in this context. In other words... to declare that you have God's provision and protection without attending to or amending your ways and deeds... is a lie. It's fraudulent activity as far as God is concerned.

"Will you steal, murder, commit adultery, swear falsely, make offerings to Baal, and go after other gods that you have not known, and then come and stand before me in this house, which is called by my name, and say 'We are delivered!' – only to go on doing all these abominations?" Jeremiah 7:9-10

The nation's religious practices are being revealed as an empty charade. Nothing about their lives would indicate they even believe in God, let alone worship Him. They were living lives no different than all of the other nations around them, yet somehow still believed that as they came together for worship at the temple, all was ok. They collectively would shout, "We are saved!"

"Has this house, which is called by my name, become a den of robbers to you?" Jeremiah 7:11

It's a good thing that has changed.

＊

I grew up mostly in Southern Baptist Churches. When we went to church, everyone wore their "Sunday best", we sang from a hymnal, the preacher delivered a lot of "fire and brimstone", and concluded with the requisite 5-minute altar call singing through the entirety of "Just As I Am". My favorite was the Sunday afternoon potlucks in the fellowship hall. Immediately following church, we'd all cram into the large room at the opposite end of the building that was set up with those white portable rectangular tables and the grey metal folding chairs. Soon, there were so many adults talking and "fellowshipping" that no one noticed a 10-year-old boy having dessert as a three-course meal. Sister Edna's banana pudding was the perfect appetizer to Sister Bea's main course of sweet potato pie, polished off with Sister Shaw's cherry cobbler and a scoop of Brother Tom's homemade vanilla ice cream – to God be the glory, great things He hath done! By the time we got home, the impending sugar crash would send me hurtling towards my bed for the obligatory Sunday afternoon nap.

However, it wasn't all pies and rainbows. Due to my dad's para-military employment, we moved about every three years. Here is a short list of events that occurred at the many churches we attended during my growing up years: A pastor was fired for having an affair with the secretary; a girl who was new to our church told me how the youth pastor from her previous church had told he loved her and kissed her on the mouth – she was 15; Our youth pastor was released for "theological differences" with the main pastor, only to be replaced by a man who was engaged to the main pastor's daughter; Ironically, that new youth pastor wasn't our youth pastor very long before the main pastor's daughter turned up pregnant – prior to the wedding. There was a very public and very painful procedure of church discipline that happened after that event. At the time it seemed completely unnecessary and cruel, however as an adult I see why it was done and grateful we had a pastor who was willing to be faithful.

These are not incidents isolated to the churches I went to. Churches are made up of humans. Imperfect humans who are prone to making mistakes. However, if corrective action is not immediately taken when those mistakes occur, the problems fester, grow, and become systemic. There are many examples.

On February 10th, 2019, a news story broke in the Houston Chronicle and San Antonio Express-News that revealed a long-term sexual abuse scandal in Southern Baptist churches. Approximately 380 pastors and church volunteers faced accusations of sexual misconduct, which left over 700 victims in their wake. It came to light that the Southern Baptist Convention actively worked to cover up the allegations.

From the late 1980s to the early 2000s there were repeated revelations about decades of abuse and cover up occurring within the Catholic Church against mostly boys between the ages of 11 and 14.

A 2017 report by Lifeway Research uncovered the fact that 1 in 10 American churches has experienced embezzlement.

In 2023, the Church of Jesus Christ of Latter-Day Saints was fined heavily by the Securities and Exchange Commission for using a series of shell companies to hide billions of dollars from the public over two decades. "We allege that the LDS Church's investment manager, with the Church's knowledge, went to great lengths to avoid disclosing the Church's investments..." The purpose behind this activity was to hide the scale of the Church's holdings, which exceeded $100 million. One whistleblower said, "...the reason the Church sought to conceal its wealth was to ensure continued tithing by believers."

Willard Leonard Jones, pastor of Greater Cornerstone Baptist Church in Oklahoma, received a 37-month prison term for embezzling nearly $1 million from a community center he founded that was meant to serve he church's surrounding neighborhood. Instead, Jones used funds for his personal mortgage payments, his gambling habit and other luxuries.

Not to mention scandals associated with pastors Bill Hybels, Carl Lentz, James McDonald, Brian Houston, and Mark Driscoll – both individually and as a collective – we aren't that much different than the worshippers we read about in Jeremiah.

May I have permission to be direct with you?

It isn't just our leaders. We gather in well-furnished, beautiful sanctuaries, sing along with amazing worship, and affirm the historical creeds of the church. All the while, many of us live with hidden sin, unrepentant hearts, and lives that reflect no real intention of being aligned with the gospel.

Proximity to the holy does not equate to holiness. Attendance, ritual, and tradition do not deliver salvation. Jeremiah's warning cuts across the centuries: We cannot live lives of indulgent, unrepentant sin and expect the house of God to be our shelter. If the temple in Jerusalem can become a den of robbers – so can my church. So can your church.

❁

"Has this house, which is called by my name, become a den of robbers to you?" Jeremiah 7:11

The Hebrew word for "my name" is *shem*. It carries the connotation of reputation and character. Today, you and I might say "he has a good name", which we interpret to mean that person is trustworthy. By using this term, God is expressing concern for his reputation that is being tarnished by the activity of the Israelites.

What is the reputation and character of God according to scripture?

> "The LORD, the LORD, a God merciful and gracious, slow to anger, and abounding in steadfast love and faithfulness." Exodus 34:6

God is loving and compassionate. He commands the Israelites, as his representatives in the world, to be the same way:

> "You shall not wrong a sojourner or oppress him... You shall not mistreat any widow or fatherless child. If you do mistreat them... I will hear their cry, and my wrath will burn..." Exodus 22:21-24

> "You shall love your neighbor as yourself." Leviticus 19:18

> "You shall treat the stranger who sojourns with you as the native among you, and you shall love him as yourself..." Leviticus 19:33-34

> "Whoever despises his neighbor is a sinner, but blessed is he who is generous to the poor." Proverbs 14:21

"Learn to do good; seek justice, correct oppression; bring justice to the fatherless, plead the widow's cause." Isaiah 1:17

God commands the nation of Israel to love those nations around them and to pay special attention to the most vulnerable in society. He tells them this is for a specific reason: "...you shall remember that you were a slave in Egypt and the LORD your God redeemed you from there; therefore I command you to do this." Deuteronomy 24:18

God had moved toward the Israelites in compassion and love to save them from their slavery in Egypt. Now, as God's representatives, they were to be the same way in the world and in so doing, show the nations what God was like. Yet, instead of being others-focused, their focus had turned inward and they began to live for themselves and their own prosperity and in the process neglected those that God cared about. *This is very serious business to God.*

What do you know about the ancient city of Sodom and why it was destroyed? You are probably familiar with the story a bit – this is where Lot lived, and they were allowed to escape before God destroyed it, and they were told as they were leaving not to look back, but Lot's wife did and was turned into a pillar of salt. This was a city that was declared in scripture to be exceedingly wicked.

In Genesis 13:13 we have this description:

"Now the men of Sodom were wicked, great sinners against the LORD." That's how it reads in English. Transliterated Hebrew is much harsher: "Men of Sodom – wicked reprobates of small worth and sinners toward Yahweh exceedingly". Can it get much worse? What were they doing in Sodom that was so offensive to God?

I had been taught that the city was destroyed due to the deep homo-sexual sin occurring which was detestable to God. After all, this is where the term sodomy originates. But is that accurate? Is that the reason God wiped it off the map? Regardless of what you have been told, there is only one verse in the bible where *God himself* declares the reasons he destroyed them:

> "Behold, this was the guilt of your sister Sodom: she and her daughters had pride, excess of food, and prosperous ease, but did not aid the poor and needy. They were haughty and did an abomination before me. So I removed them, when I saw it." Ezekiel 16:49-50

Sodom was judged for its self-centered prosperity, social injustice, and moral arrogance. They had plenty, but no compassion. They refused to reflect God's heart for the needy.

❋

In our rush to judgement its helpful to pause and consider the question of intention. Did the nation of Israel, the Southern Baptist Convention, the Catholic Church, the Church of Jesus Christ of Latter-day Saints, or any of the other examples mentioned start out with the intention of being a place or people of corruption and cover-up? Of course not. Like any gradual descent, individual compromises or changes over time seem small and insignificant at first; they are often overlooked or rationalized away until the situation has escalated to a point where it's much harder to reverse course.

Paul details in Romans how the slow slide into moral corruption happens, and it begins simply: "For although they knew God, they did not honor Him as God, or give thanks to Him..." (1:21a). Not honoring God as God just means that He is not sitting on the throne of your heart. He is not the most important thing in your life. There are many things that compete for first place in our affections. Good things. Our spouse, our children, our jobs. But scripture is saying that only God can occupy that space because He is the only one who can bear the weight of the expectations you place on the thing you love most. I have found it takes great daily intention to place God at the center of my affections.

The second step downward is "...they did not...give thanks to Him." (1:21a) Cultivating a heart of gratitude helps us to realize that we have many things to be thankful for, much of which we did nothing to earn.

When God is no longer truly God in our lives, we become less grateful, then what? "...they became futile in their thinking, and their foolish hearts were darkened." (1:21b)

When we refuse to honor God as God, and refuse to give Him thanks, our thinking becomes "futile" – in Greek this word means "to render pointless". It is a passive word that means "it just happens over time that your thinking becomes the thinking of a fool". After this, "...their foolish hearts were darkened." God's light in your life is obscured. Do you see the steps downward that are happening here?

When we no longer place God as the priority in our lives, giving thanks to Him for his goodness, our thinking over time will begin to become more foolish, and the light of God in our lives becomes obscured.

What happens next? "Claiming to be wise, they became fools..." (1:22). We grow in pride and become wise in our own eyes. Pride is the burden of a foolish person.

The result? They stop worshipping God:

> "...and (they) exchanged the glory of the immortal God
> for images resembling mortal man and birds and animals
> and creeping things."

Things begin to pick up speed now as we read "Therefore God gave them up in the lusts of their hearts to impurity..." (1:24); "For this reason God gave them up to dishonorable passions." (1:26); and finally "And since they did not see fit to acknowledge God, God gave them up to a debased mind to do what ought not to be done." (1:28)

God gave them up... God gave them up... God gave them up.

God will ultimately let you have what you want. If you go down that path long enough, He will eventually stop trying to redirect you and let you have what you have been pushing for.

The results are disastrous:

> "They were filled with all manner of unrighteousness, evil,
> covetousness, malice. They are full of envy, murder, strife,
> deceit, maliciousness. They are gossips, slanderers, haters
> of God, insolent, haughty, boastful, inventors of evil, dis-
> obedient to parents, foolish, faithless, heartless, ruthless."
> (1:29-31)

All of this began by simply not honoring God as God.

My concern in this chapter is not one of intention. As Christians, I think we all *want* to honor God as God, both individually and collectively as a church.

My concern is that somewhere along the way, we unintentionally lost the plot.

In many places, we have become skilled at looking the part while neglecting the deeper calling of God's people. In our zeal to be relevant, we know how to draw a crowd, how to program, how to create moments that move people – but how often has that resulted in life transformation? The state of the American Church would indicate we have a tendency to elevate charisma over character and growth in attendance versus growth in godliness. We have built ministries that attract the masses, but struggle to cultivate holiness. And like in Jeremiah's day, we as individuals live compartmentalized lives and assume that because we attend church each Sunday and a small group during the week that God is pleased. Have we bought into the deceptive words: "The temple of the LORD, the temple of the LORD, the temple of the LORD"?

God can tell the difference between shallow ritual and true devotion.

This may feel like an accusation, but it is an invitation. And please know, I'm writing to myself first.

Every believer carries the name of Christ. And with that name comes both great privilege and sacred responsibility. We are called to reflect His character—to live as people marked by grace, humility, and love for the vulnerable. To care about what He cares about. To show the world what God is like, not just through our words, but through our lives.

There's grace here. Not condemnation.

The story of Scripture is filled with return. Again and again, God's people stray—and again and again, God calls them back. Not to shame them, but to restore them. Not to erase them, but to re-form them. That same invitation is open today. For churches, for leaders, for ordinary believers—for all of us. If we've drifted, we can return. If we've grown cold, we can ask for renewal. If we've forgotten what matters most, we can remember.

The Lord's words to Jeremiah still ring true for us today: "Amend your ways and your deeds... then I will let you dwell in this place" (Jer. 7:3). See God's warning for what it is – mercy extended. He does not delight in condemnation, but in restoration. Our churches do not have to be dens of robbers. They can become houses of prayer, havens of healing, communities where justice flows like a river and righteousness like a never-failing stream. But for that to happen, we must repent. We must return—not just with words, but with lives that reflect His heart.

The question remains: will we?

CHAPTER SIX

ON A WING AND A PRAYER

"AND JESUS SAID 'WHO WAS IT THAT TOUCHED ME?'" LUKE 8:45

One of my favorite pastimes is learning the history behind idioms in the English language. As a refresher, idioms are expressions where the meaning of the phrase is different from the literal meaning of the individual words. For example, when we say "let the cat out of the bag", we are not literally releasing a feline from a sack. The idiom means to reveal a secret that was supposed to be kept hidden. The origin story of the phrase has to do with a punishment device used by the Royal Navy known as the "cat o'nine tails". The leather whip had cords with knots that, when used to punish a sailor, would leave severe scratches on his back. The device, being leather, had to be kept in a bag to protect it from drying out in the salty air. Thus, if someone reported a sailor for committing an offense that would result in this type of punishment, he was said to have "let the cat out of the bag."

I was first introduced to the idiom "on a wing and a prayer" when listening to the theme song of one of my favorite television shows of the early 80's– The Greatest American Hero. It's about an ordinary school teacher named Ralph Hinkley who encounters aliens that give him a red and black suit that, when worn, gives him superhuman capabilities. Ralph was somewhat hapless and, true to form, lost the instruction manual for the suit. The show was a comedy-drama, and the comedy part came from Ralph having to learn how to use the suit through trial and error – mostly error. The theme song became a hit on the radio, and I had the 45. Part of the song goes "... flying away on a wing and a prayer, who could it be? Believe it or not, it's just me..." I listened to that song over and over. I wanted to be like that – an ordinary hero. A normal-looking kid who could do amazing things. I wanted to be Ralph Hinkley. Then one day I asked my mom, "What does he mean... 'on a wing and a prayer'?" She said, "It means he doesn't have a good chance of success". After that, I no longer wanted to be Ralph Hinkley.

The idiom "on a wing and a prayer" is used to describe being in a bad situation and that success is riding on pure luck or dependent upon God Himself intervening. The phrase originated during World War II and first appeared in the 1942 film, *The Flying Tigers,* when John Wayne's character (Captain Jim Gordon) asks a hotel clerk about an incoming flight that contained a group of replacement pilots: "Any word on that flight yet?" The hotel clerk responds: "Yes sir, it was attacked and fired upon by Japanese aircraft. She's coming in on one wing and a prayer." The next year, songwriters Harold Adamson and Jimmie McHugh wrote the song *Comin' in on a Wing and a Prayer*, which tells the tale of a damaged military plane with one engine limping back home. Over time, the phrase became a popular idiom in English in the United States.

When the situation is dire, and it appears there is no hope – sometimes all you have is a wing and a prayer.

⬧

Even though we have discussed many Hebrew words thus far, we haven't covered something more fundamental to the Hebrew language. Biblical Hebrew is considered a "poor" language. By that I mean it simply doesn't have very many words; only approximately 8,000. Now, before you start thinking that sounds like a lot, the Oxford English Dictionary lists over 171,000 words. English is a very "rich" language. Because we have so many words in English, we can be very specific when we are defining something. For example, take the English word "love". Now consider all of the words we have that convey all the aspects of love. Just a sampling includes: Affection, adoration, devotion, passion, attraction, care, endearment, compassion, and tenderness.

Because Hebrew is a "poor" language, instead of *many words* that mean one thing, one word can mean *many things*. For instance, take the Hebrew word for "good", which is *tov*. *Tov* can mean good, goodness, good things, prosperity, beauty, moral excellence, a desirable quality, and tangible blessings. One additional feature of Hebrew is that a word can not only mean each one of these things, it often means *all of them*. Kind of a both/and situation. Think of the Hebrew language as that time you were determined to get all of your belongings for a week of travel into your carry-on bag. Each Hebrew word is like an overstuffed suitcase – it can mean one thing or another and often means *both*.

In this chapter, we are looking at the first question we have analyzed from the New Testament, which was originally written in Greek (as this was the language of the world at the time). However, because the characters in the story are Israelites, when discussing translations, we will take the Greek words behind our English version for better understanding and, at times, look at the Hebrew equivalent when necessary. If this seems confusing, it will become clear with an example later in the chapter.

●

"And Jesus said 'Who was it that touched me? Luke 8:45

To set the scene for this question, Jesus is likely within his second year of a three year-ministry. By this point, Jesus has become quite popular among the people and is starting to draw the interest of those in power. Jesus' ministry is iterant which just means he is on the move a lot. He will go from town to town, not staying very long in one place. He had already given the "Sermon on the Mount", calmed the storm, raised a child from the dead, and was performing healings everywhere he went. Of course, this drew large crowds that would follow him from town to town.

The scene that prompts Jesus' question is detailed in Matthew 9, Mark 5, and Luke 8. We will lean primarily on Mark and Luke's account.

After healing a demon-possessed man on the eastern side of the Sea of Galilee (the Decapolis), Jesus and his disciples got into a boat and crossed back to the northwestern side of the sea, where the towns of Capernaum and Bethsaida were located. This area was "home base" for much of Jesus' ministry.

"And when Jesus had crossed again in the boat to the other side, a great crowd gathered about him, and he was beside the sea. Then came one of the rulers of the synagogue, Jairus by name, and seeing him, he fell at his feet and implored him earnestly, saying, 'My little daughter is at the point of death. Come and lay your hands on her, so that she may be made well an live.' And he went with him."
Mark 5:21-24

While Jesus is attending to the crowd, possibly teaching, possibly healing, this man Jairus begs Jesus to come heal his "little daughter" who was "at the point of death". Jesus goes. What do you think the crowd overhearing this decided to do? Anxious to see another miracle, they went right along with them.

"And a great crowd followed him and thronged about him." Mark 5:24

"As Jesus went, the people pressed around him." Luke 8:42

The Greek word used in Mark for "thronged" is *sunthlibo*, meaning "pressed together". The word "pressed" in Luke is the Greek word *sumpnigo*, which means "to strangle completely" – obviously being used in a figurative sense in this verse. In context, these words refer to a physical convergence so tight that normal movement is not possible. Think of the last time you saw footage of someone famous or infamous trying to make their way through a crowd, and the media and cameras are pressing in on them, so much so that typically authorities are needed to clear a path just so they can walk to where they are going. That is the scene here.

Somewhere in this heaving mob of people is a woman whose backstory has her so desperate she would do anything to get close to this man at the center of the throng.

> "And there was a woman who had had a discharge of blood for twelve years, and who had suffered much under many physicians, and had spent all that she had, and was no better but rather grew worse." Mark 5:25-26

❀

It was New Year's Eve, December 31st, 2020. I was at home with my ten-year-old daughter Rachel. Up until this point in her life, she had not stayed up until midnight to "watch the ball drop", and this year she was determined to do so. As you likely recall, this was in the middle of the COVID crisis. We hadn't been impacted by it as a family, but there were no public New Year's Eve celebrations, or any friends having any parties for obvious reasons. Rachel and I made the most of it, playing games, eating snacks and singing Karaoke into the nighttime hours. Around 10pm, we were sitting on the couch watching the virtual celebration – a surreal scene of an abandoned Time Square – as no spectators were allowed to gather in person. Rachel laid her head in my lap and we waited for the ball to drop. When it did, I leaned over and said "Happy New Year!" to find that Rachel had fallen asleep. When I woke her and kissed her forehead, I thought she felt unusually warm. She said "I don't feel very good..." and I got the thermometer... 100 degrees. I gave her some acetaminophen and put her to bed, hoping and praying she hadn't gotten "the 'rona".

Rachel has traditionally been an early riser – typically up by 6 am. When she didn't come down by 7, I went up to her room to check on her. Temperature 104, severe aches and a strange rash all over her upper torso. A trip to Children's Hospital confirmed it was COVID. Under CDC protocol, this meant Rachel had to be isolated for at least 10 days. That meant Rachel would be in a separate room, with no shared meals. I was not to be within 6 feet of her, and if I had to be, I must be wearing a mask and not come in contact with her. Additionally, as someone who had close contact with her, I had to be in quarantine for 14 days.

My bedroom was downstairs and Rachel's was upstairs. She had access to her own bathroom and a play area in our upstairs loft. So physically, it was easy for us to maintain the CDC isolation recommendation. Emotionally, it was a very different matter. The pained expression on her face when I would come upstairs to bring her food with my mask on, setting down her food on her bed while trying my best to keep my distance, was almost too much to bear. 10 days with no hugs, no bedtime prayer, no shared meals, no games. The upstairs loft overlooked the living room. She would sit on the floor looking down through the balusters, and we would have conversations from 30 feet away. It looked like she was in a cell behind those spindles. For all intents and purposes, she was.

Eventually, after a few days, the rash cleared, the fever went away, and we were counting the remaining days left to complete her isolation. I still remember that first hug after her isolation period ended that brought tears to both of our eyes.

And that was just 10 days.

●

"And there was a woman who had a discharge of blood for
12 years..." Mark 5:25

One of the things that inhibits our understanding of scripture is our
relative ignorance of ancient Near Eastern cultural norms. We can read a
verse like this and think, "Poor woman. It's hard to deal with any ongoing
medical issue." While that would be a true statement, it badly misses the
mark of what this woman would have experienced over those 12 years.

Due to the phrasing in Greek, scholars believe this woman is suffering
from chronic bleeding caused by a gynecological condition such as men-
orrhagia. According to Levitical law, this would have made her ceremo-
nially "unclean" while she was bleeding. This meant that everything she
touched would become unclean, and anyone who touched her became
unclean. (Leviticus 15:25-27) The ramifications of this are dramatic. She
would not be able to enter the temple or participate in religious life; She
could not touch others, and they could not touch her; No shared meals...
no embraces... no physical affection... for 12 years. Twelve *years*. The
time frame involved would also mean no marriage (or abandonment if
she was once married).

"She had suffered much under many physicians, and had
spent all that she had, and was no better but rather grew
worse." Mark 5:26

To compound matters, the woman was ruined financially by trying everything possible to heal her condition. Ostracized, spiritually isolated, and now impoverished.

The situation is dire, and there appears to be no hope.

She has tried everything she can think of to cure her condition and has suffered the loss of everything in the process. She cannot have children, cannot have a husband, cannot be around her family... she may be alive, but what is her identity? Not a mother, a wife, a child... she is an outcast, shunned by society. Unwanted and without value.

But now, whether she has sought him out or happens to be there when he is going by, she suddenly finds herself in proximity to this man Jesus and the large crowd he has attracted.

"She had heard the reports about Jesus..." Mark 5:27

She has heard the rumors of a man named Jesus of Nazareth who has been traveling around teaching and healing people. Even though she was a social outcast, *everyone* had heard the stories about this man. Some have said he is a prophet, like Elijah – powerful in word and deed – with the ability to perform miracles. Some even believe he is the messiah. They are saying he has healed the blind, caused cripples to walk again... even raised the dead! More than that, she has heard that he isn't afraid to be near people like her. In fact, she heard that he healed someone with leprosy by touching him... *touching him!!*

What if the rumors about this man Jesus are true? What if he is not just a healer or a prophet, but the actual messiah? A glimmer of hope illuminates the darkness, and she makes a decision to act.

"She came up behind him and touched the fringe of his garment..." Luke 8:44

"For she said, if I touch even his garments, I will be made well." Mark 5:28

Remember the crowd pressing in around Jesus. This woman isn't just sneaking up behind him; she would have needed to actively push and pull her way through the crowd to get close to Jesus – making everyone she touches unclean in the process. She is risking shame and serious punishment by her bold and desperate move. She isn't even trying to get all the way to the man himself; she is just trying to get *close enough to grab the edge of his shirt.*

On the surface, her actions may seem reckless and frantic, but they actually reveal something else altogether. This is a woman of deep faith who is well acquainted with scripture.

●

Let's take a moment and discuss basic first-century fashion in the ancient Near East. Typically, in that day, men would wear an "inner garment" and an "outer garment". The inner garment would have been a long tunic (a long shirt) that was made of wool or linen, and would have been worn next to the skin. The outer garment was then placed over the tunic, providing modesty, warmth, and potentially signaling social status.

When it came to this outer garment, God had something peculiar he commanded the Israelites to add to it:

"The LORD said to Moses, 'Speak to the people of Israel, and tell them to make tassels on the corners of their garments throughout their generations, and to put a cord of blue on the tassel of each corner. And it shall be a tassel for you to look at and remember all the commandments of the LORD, to do them, not to follow after your own heart and your own eyes...'" Numbers 15:37-39

"You shall make yourself tassels on the four corners of the garment with which you cover yourself." Deuteronomy 22:12

The Hebrew name for these tassels is *tzitzit* (pronounced "zeet zeet"). These braided appendages would hang down from the four corners of the outer garment as a visible reminder of the commandments of the Lord, and are still worn by Torah observant Jews today.

The Greek word (used in the New Testament) for *tzitzit* (the tassels) is *kraspedon*. In Luke 8:44, we read that "she came up behind him and touched the fringe (*kraspedon*) of his garment...".

So the woman in this story is *specifically reaching for one of the tassels on Jesus' garment*. What about the tassel is so important that it becomes the focal point of her attempt to be healed?

Its not *what* the tassel is as much as *where* the tassel is located.

❋

The historical peak of the nation of Israel is during the 40-year reign of King David. Under David, the nation was at maximum political and military strength, and the religious fidelity of David was the greatest of any King prior to or after. God made a covenant with David in 2 Samuel 7:12-13 "I will raise up your offspring after you... and I will establish the throne of his kingdom forever." This covenant planted the seed of Israel's expectation of a "Son of David" who would reign *forever*. This future king was referred to as the Messiah. After the death of David, the kingdom began its slide into idolatry and eventually captivity. Even in the midst of these dark days, while the prophets warned of judgment, they also prophesied a future king, a Messiah:

> "For to us a child is born, to us a son is given; and the government shall be upon his shoulder, and his name shall be called Wonderful Counselor, Mighty God, Everlasting Father, Prince of Peace. Of the increase of his government and of peace there will be no end, on the throne of David and over his kingdom, to establish it and to uphold it with justice and with righteousness from this time forth and forevermore." Isaiah 9:6-7

By Jesus' day, Israel was occupied by Rome and ruled through local kings and governors who were loyal to Rome. Messianic hope during this time was at a fever pitch, and surely discussion of the many prophecies that related to the coming Messiah were not only well known by the Jews but likely a frequent topic of discussion and conversation.

One of those prophecies is from Malachi 4:2 (God is speaking):

> "But for you who fear my name, the sun of righteousness shall rise with healing in his wings..."

The Hebrew word for "wings" is *kanaf*. The imagery of God having wings is prevalent in the Old Testament and is often used when describing divine refuge, protection, and power.

> "He will cover you with his feathers, and under his wings you will find refuge; his faithfulness will be your shield and rampart." Psalm 91:4

> "Keep me as the apple of your eye; hid me in the shadow of your wings." Psalm 17:8

> "You yourselves have seen what I did to Egypt, and how I carried you on eagles' wings and brought you to myself." Exodus 19:4

Recall the point made earlier, that as a poor language, Hebrew words can have multiple meanings. An interesting thing about the word *kanaf* is that in addition to "wing" it also means... "corner".

Thus, the messianic prophecy can also be rendered "... the sun of righteousness will rise with healing in his corners (*kanaf*)..."

Why does the woman reach out for the tassel of Jesus' garment? "The LORD said to Moses, 'Speak to the people of Israel, and tell them to make tassels on the corners (*kanaf*) of their garments...'" The tassels are located on the *kanaf*.... the corner. She knows that if Jesus is the Messiah, healing is found in his wings – in his corners.

She is a woman who knows the text.

She takes her knowledge and puts it into action by forcing her way through the crowd and touching the corner, the wing, the *kanaf* of his garment.

> "And immediately the flow of blood dried up, and she felt
> in her body that she was healed of her disease." Mark 5:29

Amazing. She reaches out in faith and is "healed of her disease."

But wait. Why does Mark put it this way?

Why not just say "she was healed"? After all, he has already told us in detail what her issue was, why she believed Jesus could heal her, and the specific actions she took. It would have been just as clear to say "...and she felt in her body that she was healed", and we all would understand it. Yet he takes the opportunity to highlight that she was healed *of her disease.*

Is it possible that this woman is in need of more than just her disease being healed? Consider her 12-year isolation and its likely impacts. Her heart has been homeless, her spirit trampled, her emotions repressed, and she has been physically isolated from her family and community for over a decade. What would that do to a person? What would that do to you?

The only identity someone like that would have in this society would be that of a nameless, faceless pariah to be avoided at all costs. To the community, nothing else about her matters.

Thankfully, that's not all that matters to God.

> "And Jesus said, 'Who was it that touched me?' When
> all denied it, Peter said, 'Master, the crowds surround you
> and are pressing in on you!' But Jesus said, 'Someone

touched me, for I perceive that power has gone out of me.'" Luke 8:45-46

The crowd is a throng about Jesus. This woman pushes her way in from behind to get just close enough to touch the corner of his garment. When she does, she is healed. No one ever needs to know she was there. With the large crowd that is headed to Jairus' house to heal his daughter from near death, you could forgive all of them for sensing that there isn't any time to waste concerning themselves with who is or is not touching Jesus. Surely there were many touching him, some intentionally, some inadvertently.

But Jesus stops the parade and asks the question, 'Who touched me?' and if he is God incarnate, he already knows the answer to it. No one is willing to admit that they did, since "all denied it". (All being one of those words in Greek that means... all. Which included the now healed woman.) Peter makes the statement we all would make "Umm... Jesus, the crowd is surrounding you and pressing in on you... what do you mean 'Who touched me?' They ALL touched you!"

※

At our 7th-grade basketball awards banquet, I certainly wasn't expecting to get an award. It was my first year playing basketball, and while I had improved, I still rode the bench and only played when games were out of reach. So as the team stood up with our coach at the front of the auditorium and he began to hand out awards, I just waited for it all to be over. Team MVP – Trent Climpson; Most Improved – Jarrod Bench; Leadership Award – Shawn Harmon. Before handing out each award, the coach would say a few things about the player before giving their name, and at some point, those of us on the team knew who he was speaking about before he announced the winner to the audience. Not many in the crowd did because you had to have some inside knowledge to know who the coach was describing.

The final award was something called "The Coaches Award". As the coach began to describe the teammate to receive this award, at first I had no clue who he was talking about. "... this player outworked all of our other players..." That could be either Scott Adams or Jeff Byers – known gym rats. "This player always kept a positive attitude and became a real leader on our team..." That could also be Jeff Byers or maybe Erick Moseley – he was the life of the team emotionally. But as the coach shared more examples of situations in practice and games involving this player I started to realize.. he is talking about *me*. Me? My eyes darted to the floor, and I felt my face getting flush. The coach was talking about me, and most of the people in the room didn't know. But he knew who he was describing, and I knew who he was describing. And the rest of the time he spoke, I felt like he was speaking directly to me. There might as well not have been anyone else in the room.

◉

Jesus knows who touched him. The woman knows it was her. At first, she denies it – "When *all* denied it..." Yet when she saw she wasn't going to be able to receive anonymous healing, she stepped forward.

> "And when the woman saw that she was not hidden, she came trembling, and falling down before him declared in the presence of all the people why she had touched him, and how she had been immediately healed." Luke 8:47

Notice that Jesus, although he knows who she is, doesn't call her out. He invites her forward. It is clear from the text that the woman had hoped to complete this act in secret, but when she saw that was not possible, she came forward. Mark intentionally provides us details about this... "she came trembling"... "declared in the presence of all the people"... "why she had touched him"... "how she had been immediately healed."

What is important about these details? Why is it important to Jesus that she publicly out herself in front of "all the people" as having been "immediately healed"?

Jesus saw beyond her need of simply being healed *of her disease.* Her heart needed healing, and the only way that was going to happen was to be reconciled to the community that had long since forgotten her as an outcast. In asking her to come forward, Jesus facilitates that reconciliation and sets in motion the healing process *for her soul.*

But Jesus isn't done yet. There is one more thing.

> "And he said to her, 'Daughter, your faith has made you
> well, go in peace.'" Luke 8:48

He reminds her of her true identity. This is the only occurrence in Scripture of Jesus directly referring to another person as "daughter". She is a beloved daughter of the Most High.

Close your eyes for a moment – try your best to consider all she has been through. For 12 years, no one has called her anything but "unclean". Now imagine what it must have been like for her when Jesus looked on her, as you would one of your own children, and called her "daughter".

All accomplished when the situation couldn't have been more desperate or dire.

Truly on a "wing" and a prayer.

❂

The heart of this story is the heart of the gospel.

Because the truth is, many of us are like that woman. Carrying wounds we'd rather keep hidden. Searching all the while in quiet desperation for a touch of relief without the risk of exposure. Healing without revealing. Miracles without vulnerability.

But Jesus sees. He knows. He calls us out – not to embarrass us, but to embrace us.

Because Jesus doesn't ask for perfect faith. He honors persistent faith. Reaching faith. Faith that dares to push through the crowd.

God wants to go beyond healing to wholeness.

And that's good news for those of us today who carry wounds that run deeper than our bodies. Maybe your past has made you an outcast in your family, your church, or your community. Maybe you sit at the holiday table, and no one really sees you anymore. Maybe you carry a label—"divorced," "addict," "felon," "failure"—that no one says out loud, but everyone seems to remember.

Perhaps you've even labeled yourself. When we do, it's usually with the most damaging label of all: "not enough". Not good enough, smart enough, thin enough, strong enough, rich enough, talented enough, educated enough, patient enough, attractive enough, and a million other "enoughs".

Maybe today, your faith feels like it's held together with duct tape and doubt. Maybe you're just barely flying—on one wing and a prayer.

And this story declares... *that's enough.*

The crowd may push past you. Society may press you to the margins. But Jesus will stop everything to call you forward—not to make you a spectacle, but to call you His. He doesn't just fix what's broken. He restores what was lost. Your name. Your place. Your peace.

You can never know that God is all you need until God is all you've got.

So if you feel like your faith is limping along and held together with questions and regrets – reach anyway. Reach through the shame. Reach through the fear. Reach like she did, on a wing and a prayer.

CHAPTER SEVEN

COMFORTABLY COMPLACENT

"WHEN JESUS SAW HIM LYING THERE AND KNEW THAT HE HAD ALREADY BEEN THERE A LONG TIME, HE SAID TO HIM, 'DO YOU WANT TO BE HEALED?'"
JOHN 5:6

During the summer before my 7th-grade year, we moved from Dallas, Texas, to Morrow, Georgia, which was a suburb of Atlanta. I became friends with a guy in my grade who lived in our neighborhood. Let's call him Max. He was an only child and had parents who both worked. This meant he was given almost anything he wanted, including the best and newest video games, a top-of-the-line pellet gun, and a Honda three-wheeler. Going to Max's house was like going to Six Flags. So I did. A lot.

Because Max's parents didn't come home until dinner time, he was alone a lot. Many days after school, I'd hop on my bike and ride it down the hill and around the corner to his house. We'd play video games, shoot things with his pellet gun, make prank phone calls, pop wheelies on his 3-wheeler, and anything else our unsupervised juvenile minds could think up. One day he showed me his parents liquor cabinet and, knowing where the key was, opened it up. I had an exciting rush course through my veins while I stared at all the bottles. It was like an adult's candy store. He said he would occasionally take nips out of the vodka and showed me where his parents made marks on each bottle to ensure he wasn't drinking from them. He noted after drinking how he would fill the bottle back up to the line with tap water. Max was a genius. While we didn't help ourselves to his parents' booze that day, one day soon we would.

I don't recall the exact day, only that it was a fall afternoon and we were tired of playing video games and attempting to blow up his G.I. Joe's with the "black cat" fireworks that Max always seemed to have a steady supply of. Max looked at me and said, "Hey... want to drink some of my parents' booze?" I thought of all the times my alcoholic father would pour a mixed drink for himself at the table. He did it with a level of tenderness – as if emotion was involved in mixing the concoction that would transform him, initially, into a fun-loving jokester, and later into a brooding, sharp-tongued viper. Later in life, when I heard the song "Piano Man" by Billy Joel, I knew just what he meant when describing a man at the bar who was "making love to his tonic and gin." That's what was happening. My dad *was* making love to his whiskey and Coke. Over the years he would let me sip his beer or taste his mixed drink briefly, but truthfully, I always wondered what it would be like to imbibe relentlessly, as he did.

Now I had my chance.

Max pulled out the bottle of vodka, poured some into a glass, mixed it with Sprite and handed it to me. I noticed he only poured one glass –

"Hey, aren't you having some?" I said. "No way man... my parents will be home in two hours. I can't risk that!" Oddly, this same risk never crossed my mind. I lifted the glass to my mouth and could smell the acrid smell I had detected on my father's breath so very many times. I paused for a moment. Just long enough for Max to say, "Come on man!" Honestly, I didn't need his encouragement. This was a moment I had thought about before, but I just didn't think it would come this early in life, and I was savoring the moment, so to speak.

I opened wide and downed the entire glass in two gulps. I felt the burn of the vodka hit the back of my throat and quickly wash its way down my esophagus. I had an instantaneous urge to puke, which I quelled for the moment. I turned to Max and said, "Another". He said, "Not yet; let's go sit down on the couch and see how you feel in a few minutes." In only a couple of minutes, I was feeling the rush. It felt like there was a helium balloon in my head that was wanting to pull my skull free of my neck. My cheeks felt warm. I felt internally... happy? Whatever it was, it felt glorious. I wanted more of those feelings that terrible tasting liquid gave me. The next few hours was something of a blur as Max made me two more drinks. I recall talking on the phone to a girl I had a crush on, racing through his back yard on foot while he chased me on his 3-wheeler, and Max telling me I had to leave because his parents would be home any minute. I remember Max giving me a stale candy cane from last year's Christmas tree, poking it into my mouth while he pushed me outside towards my bicycle that was lying in the grass. He said "Get out of here – that candy cane will help mask the smell of the booze."

I got on my bike and rode the half mile home in a daze. I was relieved to see that my father's truck was not in the driveway meaning he hadn't made it home from work yet. I rode my bike into the back gate, dropped it in the grass, ran the steps up to our back porch, and slid the glass door open to our living room. I could smell dinner being made, and my mom yelled, "Hello Bryan!" I mumbled, "Hi, mom" as I hustled passed her and said, "I don't feel well, I'm headed to my room." I managed to run upstairs and collapse on the bed without her asking any questions.

I woke up a couple of times but rolled over and went back to sleep, waking up to my 6am alarm to get up for school the next day. When I went down for breakfast, if my mom had suspected or detected anything the afternoon before, she didn't mention it.

By the time I was on the bus to school, I felt a wave of relief. I had gotten away with it.

Thus began my on-again, off-again relationship with the great scourge of my life: alcohol.

❁

The setting for the question of this chapter is 1st-century Jerusalem. In the northeast corner of the city, near what is called the "sheep gate", there were two pools. These pools were lying north and south and were surrounded by four covered colonnades with a fifth colonnade that separated the two pools. There was a belief that "from time to time an angel of the Lord would come down and stir up the waters" and the first person who was able to make it into the pool after the stirring would be cured of whatever their ailment.

> "Now there is in Jerusalem by the Sheep Gate a pool, in Aramaic called Bethesda, which has five roofed colonnades. In these lay a multitude of invalids – blind, lame, and paralyzed. One man was there who had been an invalid for thirty-eight years. When Jesus saw him lying

there and knew that he had already been there a long time,
he said to him, 'Do you want to be healed?'" John 5:2-6

John tells us in verse one of this chapter that this was during a feast.
This area and the rest of Jerusalem would have been packed on such an
occasion. Jesus (with his disciples in tow), make their way to this corner
of the city where a large number of people are lying in the shade of these
covered awnings, waiting for the water to be stirred – hopeful of being
healed. We are told by John that there was a particular man there who
had been an invalid for thirty-eight years.

Almost always when Jesus heals in Scripture, the person being healed
is either seeking him out, being brought to him by others, or the healing
is done in response to a request made on someone's behalf. There are
only two times in scripture, both in John, where Jesus approaches and
heals someone without request. This is one of those times. Jesus sees
the man, knows that he has been there a long time, and approaches him
with a rather odd question:

"Do you want to be healed?"

Isn't it obvious? Just look at where the man is. Is he not lying near
the pool, just waiting for the waters to be stirred up? Isn't this evidence
of his desire to be healed?

How does the man respond?

"The sick man answered him, 'Sir, I have no one to put me
into the pool when the water is stirred up, and while I am
going another steps down before me." John 5:7

In his effort to explain why he has not yet been healed, he fails to answer Jesus' direct and simple question. What he *does not say* is more telling than what he does say. That begs the question...

Does he want to be healed?

◈

My relationship with alcohol began in earnest when, at 21 years of age, I became a police officer. It was a long tradition of police officers to gather after their shift was over for what was called "choir practice", or "c.p." for short. We would collect at someone's place, have a few drinks, and talk through the craziness of the day. And in that job, there was *always* craziness. Over time, I started to host choir practice at my apartment. I worked "deep nights" – 9pm to 7am – so when I would get off work at 7am, I would head home, shower, change, go fire up the grill and pour a drink. By 8am some of the fellas, mostly all the single guys from my shift, would be showing up. We'd sit around the grill that was placed in an open outdoor area behind my apartment as all the normal people were headed out the door for work. Imagine the scene as people passed by and saw us flipping burgers, getting rowdy, and drinking at 8:15 a.m. *almost every day*. "What a bunch of degenerates!" I'm sure they thought. If they did, they weren't that far from the truth.

Over time, like with any addiction, it took a little more whiskey to achieve the effect I desired. At some point, especially on my days off, I began to have blackouts. Waking up in my bed or on the couch, not being able to recall anything that happened beyond a certain point the previous day. While these were scary, they were few and far between... initially. Yet, that too also changed as blackouts became a regular part of my drinking episodes. I began waking up in places I didn't even *recog-*

nize, and with *people* I didn't recognize. When I would start drinking, I wouldn't (couldn't?) stop until I passed out or blacked out.

I managed to get ahold of myself and quit drinking for a period of time. Eventually, the pressures and stresses of life would mount, and I would go back to the bottle for relief. After 6 years at the P.D., I left police work and began a career in financial services. During this time, I would go through long stretches without drinking. 18 months here, 2 years there. Mostly, I stopped drinking to prove to myself I wasn't an alcoholic – I didn't need to drink. Alcoholics, after all, woke up needing a drink to function, right? That wasn't me!

I had managed to move up the career ladder in financial services and had a job as a traveling salesperson, making more money than I ever thought possible for me to make – well over $500,000 per year. During one of the stretches when I was drinking, I entertained a number of work colleagues at a bar until closing. When driving back towards my hotel, my cell phone fell on the floor of my truck. I reached down to grab it and inadvertently pulled the steering wheel to the left. I crossed over the oncoming lane of traffic, down into the ditch on the other side of the road, and into a fence, narrowly missing a telephone pole. I can still see it all in slow motion. I got out of the truck and saw that the front bumper was pushed into the front left wheel. I wasn't going anywhere. In what seemed like only seconds, police were on the scene. After a brief investigation and some field sobriety tests, I was in handcuffs – arrested for DWI.

I was released the next day and went to get my truck from the pound. They pulled the bumper out from the front tire as a courtesy so I could drive it home. When I got home I let my wife know what had occurred. I was humiliated. I was scared. I thought I might lose my job. I thought I would lose the respect of my colleagues. I thought my wife my take our daughter and leave. One thing I knew *for sure* though – I was done with drinking – *forever.*

My wife recommended that I go to an AA meeting. Her recommendation felt more like an ultimatum. I found one in town and drove over to the place it was being held. I was too nervous to go in. What would it mean for me to walk through that door? What was I admitting to? The people walking through the front door didn't look anything like me. Just before putting the truck in reverse and leaving, I realized when I went home I would have to either lie to my wife, or sheepishly admit I was too much of a coward to walk in the room. I went in. I listened as each person told their story of what made them hit "rock bottom" and how AA had turned their life around. One guy I remember said that he didn't get it until his *fourth DWI*! His *fourth*!?!?! I remember thinking, "How much of an idiot do you have to be to get arrested for DWI *four times* before you realize you have a problem?"

If there is one thing I learned during that meeting, it was that I *was not* an alcoholic – *these guys had a real problem* – I just occasionally drank too much and had made a huge mistake on one night of my life. But all that was in the past. I had seen the light.

That lasted for about a year. Then the second DWI came. Then the third.

By this time, I was willing to admit that I was a "problem drinker". My biggest problem was that I liked it. I liked who I was when I was drinking. I had given myself over to the reality that once I started drinking, I wasn't going to stop until I was unconscious. That fact no longer bothered me. The few hours I would have under its spell were so wonderful, it was worth every price. I liked everything about it. If my wife had said, "It's me or the bottle" – I would have chosen the bottle. I loved the anticipation of hearing the ice land in the bottom of my tumbler. I salivated when I would pour whiskey over that ice, and I would hear it crack under the warmth of the sweet liquid. I cherished every gulp (I was long past sipping) and looked forward to the mindless oblivion it would soon induce. Like a school boy with a crush, when I wasn't drinking, I was fantasizing about drinking and thinking about when I would get to drink again. Alcohol was my lover.

Stop drinking? No, thank you. I couldn't even imagine alcohol not being a part of my life. Despite the issues it caused.

Not only did I not want to change, I couldn't see myself ever changing.

⬢

Jesus asked the man, "Do you want to be healed?" Why does Jesus ask the question? Is it even possible that the man does not actually want to be healed? Let's look at the evidence.

> "Jesus said to him, 'Get up, take up your bed, and walk.'
> And at once the man was healed, and he took up his bed and walked." John 5:8-9

Without waiting for the man to request healing, Jesus heals him and tells him to pick up his mat and walk. The man does.

> "Now that day was the Sabbath. So the Jews said to the man who had been healed, 'It is the Sabbath, and it is not lawful for you to take up your bed.' But he answered them, 'The man who healed me, that man said to me, 'Take up your bed, and walk.' They asked him, 'Who is the man who said to you, 'Take up your bed and walk?' Now

the man who had been healed did not know who it was..."
John 5:9-13

Consider that there is no record of this man thanking Jesus for healing him, though that is recorded in many other places after many other healings, and he admits to the religious leaders that he does not even know Jesus' name. If you had been overjoyed at your healing, wouldn't you have at least gotten Jesus' name? Said thank you?

> "Afterward Jesus found him in the temple and said to him, 'See, you are well! Sin no more, that nothing worse may happen to you.' The man went away and told the Jews that it was Jesus who had healed him." John 5:14-15

Now Jesus sees him in the temple and greets him. Again, instead of thanking Jesus, the man uses those two newly healed legs to trot as quickly as he can back to the religious leaders to rat Jesus out.

This is not the behavior of a man who appreciates what has just happened to him.

Why would that be? What possible explanation could there be for this man's actions?

Jesus asked the man a simple question:

"Do you want to be healed?"

It should have been obvious. The man was lying by a pool believed to possess healing power. Yet his answer wasn't a resounding "yes!" It wasn't even a yes at all. Instead, he offered a list of reasons why healing hadn't come. Excuses. Limitations. External obstacles. He didn't say, "Yes, I want to be well." He said, "I can't get there."

Maybe somewhere along the way, he had stopped wanting to be healed. After thirty-eight years of lying on that mat, it had become more than a resting place. It had become home. Healing would mean more than walking – it would mean working, relating, re-entering society, and relearning how to live. Maybe, just maybe, he wasn't ready for all that.

I wasn't either.

For years, I didn't just drink to escape. As crazy as it sounds, I drank because I liked who I became when I was drinking. Alcohol numbed the things I didn't want to feel and amplified the things I wished were true. It became more than a problem. It became my personality. My comfort. My companion. To let go of it would have meant stepping into a version of life I couldn't imagine, and at certain points did not want.

I was the man on the mat.

❋

There are psychological reasons we have an aversion to the progress healing might provide in our lives. And they're not unique to addiction.

Simple fear of the unknown keeps people in broken relationships or dead-end jobs, living unfulfilling lives. The pain we know is often less frightening than the future we don't.

Persistent failure to succeed often leads to a condition called learned helplessness. We become convinced that change is pointless. We tried once, maybe twice, and nothing changed – so why try again?

The phenomenon known as secondary gain whispers that our dysfunction *protects us*. Sometimes, we subconsciously benefit from our afflictions. For instance, staying "sick" might shield someone from responsibility, expectation, or conflict. Pain becomes protective. When this goes on long enough, people can begin to identify with their brokenness. It becomes not just something they carry – it becomes who they are. To let it go feels like a kind of death. By maintaining our brokenness, we are shielded from risk, from responsibility, from disappointment.

And slowly, that mat – whether it's a bottle, a bitterness, a secret sin, or a story we've told ourselves for years – becomes our identity.

It's not just what we're lying on.

It's who we believe we are.

But Jesus didn't ask the man if he *could* be healed. *He asked if he wanted to be.*

❊

DWI number four came on December 12, 2020. In a twist of irony only God could arrange, it happened in the town where I had been a police officer 25 years prior. Prior to this, I had been sober for 18 months after completing a Christian 12-step program. A good friend's mother had died during the COVID pandemic, and he asked me to come in town for the funeral. I did and planned on staying the night at his house. After the funeral, we went back to his place, where he was hosting a reception. In a room of the home just inside the garage, a makeshift bar had been set up with all types of liquor and beer. I decided that since I was not going anywhere (except for 50 feet down the hall to the bed I was sleeping in), it would be ok for me to have a drink or two. Of course, for someone like me, there is no such thing as having only one or two. I had several mixed drinks and was eventually picked up by a friend who took me to dinner. I had a couple of beers at dinner and the last thing I remember was getting into the passenger seat of her car. When I came to, I was lying on my side and staring at a cinder block wall in the county jail. Another blackout. Another arrest. To learn all the details, I had to wait to be bailed out of jail. It turns out my dinner companion dropped me back off at my friends house, but instead of going inside, I got in my car, eventually driving off and later to be found passed out behind the wheel at an intersection several miles away from my friends house.

"How much of an idiot do you have to be to get arrested for DWI four times before you realize you have a problem?" Now I knew the answer to that pride-filled question I had asked in my first AA meeting 8 years before. The answer was in the mirror staring back at me.

I don't know exactly why, but something changed in me over the next month. I no longer wanted this. I didn't want to be this way anymore. On January 21st of 2021, I walked through the door of an AA meeting for the first time without an ultimatum from my wife or an invitation from the county court. I walked in on my own volition because I needed to be sober.

And for the first time in my life – I *wanted* to be.

●

Do you want to be healed?

I don't know what hurts, hang-ups, addictions, setbacks, or trauma you have been through. The specifics don't matter as much as the question. Have you been able to heal from your past – even one you caused – or have you found that elusive? Is the solution to the issue perhaps more basic than you suspected?

Whatever your situation, you don't have to have it all figured out for the healing process to begin. Sometimes, it's as simple as beginning. Beginning to rise, to move, to leave behind what we thought we needed. To muster up the courage to walk through the door. But here's the thing: getting up means letting go. It means no longer lying on the mat. No longer letting it define you. No longer hiding behind the excuse. No longer holding the grudge.

Healing often is about more than just physical or emotional restoration. It is often about reforming our identity. No longer allowing the past to define us. And that can be terrifying.

Do you want to be healed?

Maybe you're not too far gone. Maybe you haven't missed your moment. Maybe you're just one question away from freedom.

Because sometimes the *real* miracle is not walking again.

It's wanting to.

CHAPTER EIGHT

SHOOT YOUR SHOT

"WHAT DO YOU WANT ME TO DO FOR YOU?" LUKE 18:41

What do you want?

Really. Take a moment, pause, and ask yourself, "What do I want?" I'll wait. Seriously. If you simply can't right now, then don't proceed with the chapter until you can take at least two minutes to reflect on this question later on. Write down your responses if possible. I will do the same.

Ok, here are my answers to the question "What do I want?" (as the answers came to me in no particular order): More commission at work; to write an insightful and impactful book; for Rachel to never have another knee surgery; to get back to 210 lbs; to be a better steward of my resources; to be more organized.

That's my list. Pretty short. Unimpressive even. And on the surface, it doesn't seem all that urgent or selfish. But when I take a step back and start asking deeper questions, such as: Why do I want this? What's underneath that desire? How would the world change if I got it? A few things come into focus.

First, most of what I want revolves around me: my comfort, my success, my sense of control.

Second, some of these aren't true desires at all; they're "shoulds." Things I tell myself I ought to want so I feel more virtuous or put together. I *should* lose weight. I *should* be a better steward of my resources. I *should* be more organized. I've had years to work on these things and taken little action.

And third, even if I got everything on this list, the world wouldn't shift very much. At best, my life might get a little easier. A little more efficient. A little more insulated.

So how about you?

If you paused and made your list – really made it – what's on it? Take a moment to read and reflect on it.

Now, ask yourself, if you got everything on your list of wants:
Who benefits?

Are they real desires or just what you think you *should* want?

Would the world change in any meaningful way?

Here's another observation I can't ignore: my list is shaped almost entirely by *my present circumstances*. Just a few months ago, some of these "wants" wouldn't have even made the list. 5 months ago was my best commission month ever, I was not seriously thinking about writing a book, and Rachel was two months away from tearing her ACL. These "wants" were not even on my radar. That alone should make me ask: Am I in touch with the *deepest* desires of my heart – or just the *loudest* ones in this moment?

The temptation for me is to read my list and think I'm doing pretty well because my list is short and docile. But what if the brevity and non-urgency of my list isn't a sign of peace or contentment, but symptomatic of a serious deficit? Of the quiet atrophy of my soul?

What if this thin little list is not a sign of health – but of a hunger I've forgotten how to feel?

●

In Luke chapter 18, Jesus, as an itinerant teacher and healer, is on the move again and nearing the ancient town of Jericho. Jericho is situated in Israel in what is known as the West Bank near the Dead Sea, and approximately 17 miles east of Jerusalem. Jericho has a significant biblical and archeological history as one of the oldest continuously inhabited cities in the world.

By this time, Jesus' renown and celebrity had grown exponentially, and large crowds followed him as he went from town to town.

> "As he (Jesus) drew near to Jericho, a blind man was sitting by the roadside, begging. And hearing the crowd going by, he inquired what this meant. They told him, 'Jesus of Nazareth is passing by.'" He cried out , "Jesus, Son of David, have mercy on me!" Luke 18:35-38

This would have been a scene similar to Chapter 5, where the woman with the "issue of blood" has heard of Jesus' reputation and forces her way through the crowd to get to Jesus in her desperate attempt to be healed. In this scene in Luke 18, the situation is more complicated as the man is blind. He won't be forcing his way through any crowd – if he is going to get an audience with Jesus, it will need to be through some other means. So he uses what he has at his disposal: "He cried out, 'Jesus, Son of David, have mercy on me!'". Let's dissect this verse in the language in which it was written to get a better mental picture of what's happening. The Greek word translated as "cried out" is *boao,* and it means to make "an urgent distress call" – it carries an intensity that refuses to be silenced.

We know the crowd surrounding Jesus is already an unusual commotion because it is what attracts the blind man's attention in the first place. To shout down the crowd, the blind man issues an intense and urgent cry using Jesus' name and the moniker "Son of David".

In that time and culture, the term "Son of David" would not have been just about ancestral lineage (though Jesus is from the line of David) – it is a term that was used for the Messiah. Similar to the woman in chapter 6 of this book, whatever this blind man has heard has led him to believe that Jesus may be the promised deliverer. In the Old Testament, there were some miracles that were prophesied to be hallmarks of the arrival of the Messiah. In particular, Isaiah, in chapters 29, 32, 35, and 42, notes that the blind will be given sight.

Knowing this, the blind man cries out.

> "And those who were in front of him rebuked him, telling
> him to be silent." Luke 18:39

Some more Greek for us. "Those who were in front" is one word in Greek *proago,* and it refers to those who were leading the way. In a crowd like this, there would need to be some people clearing the path ahead. As most of the religious leaders were not fond of Jesus, and the Roman occupiers wouldn't have made this their responsibility, who do you suppose was clearing the path for Jesus? We aren't told specifically, but I have to believe it was the disciples. Those who followed Jesus most closely to learn from him.

"Rebuked" is *epitimao* in Greek and means "to sternly warn" – they told him in no uncertain terms to shut up. Those leading the way, instead of ushering the needy blind man into Jesus' presence, are actively trying to *prevent that from happening*.

The blind man is ready to take a chance – a gamble, really – that could alter the direction of his whole life. An opportunity that could change the whole narrative. A time when he dares to believe his moment might have finally arrived. This is the window. This is the time. He takes action.

And immediately – the voices come.

The voices come not from the enemies. Not from Rome. Not from the religious elites. From the *insiders*.

The voices come to tell him to stop dreaming. Be realistic. Quiet down. Get in line. Know your place. This isn't for you. People like you don't get that kind of access. It's too late. You'll always be this way. That's not how God works.

Have you heard those voices before? They come when you start to believe your story might not be over. When you dare to pray big. When you dream that God might have something more for you.

> "But he cried out all the more, 'Son of David, have mercy on me!'" Luke 18:39

Despite the attempts to silence him, the Greek tells us that the blind man *paloos mallon krazo*. Transliterated, this phrase means that "much more than before – he was screaming and shrieking..." for mercy.

Screaming and shrieking.

This gets Jesus' attention.

> "And Jesus stopped and commanded him to be brought
> to him. And when he came near, he asked him, 'What do
> you want me to do for you?'" Luke 18:41

What an odd question. Almost annoying.

Let's say I worked for roadside assistance and you called for help. When I showed up, if you were standing by a flat left front tire, my first question isn't going to be "What do you want me to do for you?"

Knowing that Jesus is not being simply obtuse, what is going on here? Is there some other need this man has besides regaining his sight that Jesus is trying to draw his attention to?

This Greek word for "want" is *thelo,* which is a word used when a choice needs to be made and carries with it the implication that someone is ready, willing, and able to act. This isn't just a wish being made. It is a request with the certainty that it will be granted. It could be rendered "What do you *prefer* me to do for you?"

Jesus is asking him to conduct an evaluation. There are wants and then there are needs. Of all the possible things he could request, what is it he needs?

Even though Jesus knows what he will request, there is something very important about the man evaluating his options and naming his need.

> "He said, 'Lord, let me recover my sight.' And Jesus said
> to him, 'Recover your sight; your faith has made you well.'
> And immediately he recovered his sight and followed him,
> glorifying God." Luke 18:41-43a

Even in a situation this obvious, what is the importance of naming our need?

Naming our need forces us to face reality. No one in your life has lied to you more than *you* have. We are very good at deceiving ourselves. When we name it, we step into reality. We admit the truth.

Naming our need creates the space for transformation. God is not looking for perfect or even polished people – He seeks those who recognize just how broken they are.

Naming our need humbly positions us to receive grace. "God opposes the proud but gives grace to the humble" (James 4:6). Grace flows downhill – to the low places.

●

The entire idea for this book came from this question Jesus asked this blind man. When I read this scripture that summer morning, I was struck by the question. What if I were standing in front of Jesus right now, and he were to ask me "What do you want me to do for you?" What would my response be?

"To make more commission at work"?

"To write a good book"?

"To be in shape?"

"More organized in my life and my finances?"

When viewed in that light, my list is self-serving, impotent, and gutless. Are these the type of desires that would have me *screaming and shrieking* for Jesus to stop and intervene? Clearly not.

In fact, these wants are *things I can accomplish all by myself*.

Why aren't my desires radical prayers that come from the edge of desperation? No back up plan, no cushion. Why aren't I pleading with

God to do something that can't be explained, controlled or reverse-engineered?

Or why is it that when my prayers *do* sound like this, it is only when I'm out of options, overwhelmed by circumstances and reaching toward God as my last resort? Why is God always the *last* stop before I reach the end of my rope?

I don't think I'm alone in this. I'm afraid we've gotten so used to managing our own comfort that we no longer pray like people with a deep hunger for God's intervention until we have no other options left. We pray like people who are inconvenienced. As a result, our prayer lives have all the urgency of a polite grocery list.

This is *not* how we are told to pray in Scripture.

How does Jesus tell us to pray?

> "And when you pray, you must not be like the hypocrites. For they love to stand and pray in the synagogues and at the street corners, that they may be seen by others. Truly, I say to you, they have received their reward. But when you pray, go into your room and shut the door and pray to your Father who is in secret. And your Father who sees in secret will reward you. And when you pray, do not heap up empty phrases as the Gentiles do, for they think that they will be heard for their many words. Do not be like them, for your Father knows what you need before you ask him." Matthew 6:5-8

Jesus says here not to try to draw attention to yourself by praying for effect. Anyone who has prayed in public certainly has felt the weight of wanting to say the right words and, unfortunately for me at least, hoping to sound somewhat holy in the process. Jesus clearly states here that if your primary goal is to impress others, you will likely get that reward. But that is the only reward you will get. He admonishes his followers to avoid attracting attention in prayer and not to make their prayers tedious and repetitive. Then Jesus admits one of the pillars of this book – *God already knows what you need before you even ask him.* Well then if that is true, why pray? One of the answers to that is in the Greek definition of "ask" in the verse above. This word is *aiteo* in Greek and means "making a request that acknowledges the giver's authority and one's own dependence on the giver".

The kind of prayer that Jesus is talking about winds up being an admission of our complete dependence on God. Jesus is talking about the kind of prayers that don't have answers apart from God's intervention. Dangerous prayers. Prayers that can change things. Prayers that can change us.

If my prayers don't require God to act for them to be answered, then my prayers are too small. That is prayer as a good luck charm. A rabbit's foot.

Jesus actually tells his disciples how to pray. You and I call it "The Lord's Prayer", and it follows the verses in Matthew above.

"Pray then like this:

'Our Father in heaven,

hallowed be your name.

Your kingdom come,

Your will be done,

on earth as it is in heaven.

Give us this day our daily bread,

and forgive us our sins,

as we forgive those who sin against us.

And lead us not into temptation but deliver us from evil.'" Matthew 6:9-13

This prayer is dangerous. You may not feel it because you've said this prayer more than any other in your life. Familiarity renders things invisible (remember chapter one?).

First, notice this prayer does not say "*My* father in heaven... give *me* this day... forgive *me* my sins... lead *me* not... deliver *me*..." This is not a prayer centered on us as individuals. It is a prayer we are offering for and with our community.

Second, asking for God's kingdom to come is asking for His reign and rule to happen here on earth. In effect, you are pleading "God, rearrange the world I live in until it looks like yours." That is world-changing prayer. Taking yourself out of the center of your life. No longer occupying that throne. You've been a usurper to the throne long enough.

Third, we ask for our "daily bread". Not our annual bread, monthly bread, or weekly bread. The Greek word is *epiousios* – means "needful" or "only enough for today". Just what we need, and no more. This is asking God to break you of your dependence upon your material wealth for your security. To dismantle your internal idea that you are your own provider. To live in dependence on Him, not on yourself. Talk about scary.

Finally, "forgive us our sins, as we forgive those who sin against us." Don't think this means "forgive me of my sins *while I also* am forgiving those who sin against me." The Greek doesn't leave room for that interpretation. "As we" is *hos kai hemeis* in Greek and it means "in the same manner as." What we are asking God to do in this verse is for God to forgive us *in the same manner as* we forgive others. Ouch. Are you prepared for God to forgive you in the same way that you apply forgiveness? This verse is pointing out that considering all we have been forgiven of, we have no room – absolutely zero – to withhold forgiveness from another. Talk about radical.

If you are looking for a risky and daring prayer, you have it.

And don't forget the promises of prayer.

> "Whatever you ask in prayer, believe that you have received it, and it will be yours." Mark 11:24

> "Whatever you ask in my name, this I will do, that the Father may be glorified in the Son." John 14:13-14

> "If you have faith like a grain of mustard seed, you will say to this mountain, 'Move from here to there,' and it will move, and nothing will be impossible for you." Matthew 17:20

This should fuel our mountain-moving prayers with a faith and fervency built on the authority of His word.

That doesn't mean God doesn't care about all of the other things going on in our lives that impact us. Of course he does. The very hair on our heads are numbered. (Matthew 10:30)

It does mean that our wants and prayer requests might need to be re-evaluated and re-prioritized.

Regardless, Jesus still asks us the question:

What do you want me to do for you?

Not what sounds holy.

Not what feels safe.

Not what will make life a little easier.

What do you want Jesus to do for you?

The question still stands not because He doesn't know, but because naming your need does something for you. It requires humility, honesty and faith. It's you coming out of hiding, checking polite pretense at the door, and daring to believe that God still moves, still heals, still forgives and still changes things – starting with you and me.

CHAPTER NINE

THE BIGGER BARN THEORY

"BUT GOD SAID TO HIM, 'FOOL! THIS NIGHT YOUR SOUL IS REQUIRED OF YOU, AND THE THINGS YOU HAVE PREPARED WHOSE WILL THEY BE?'" LUKE 12:20

John D. Rockefeller (1839–1937), the son of a traveling peddler and a devout Baptist mother, rose from modest beginnings in Richford, New York, to become the world's first billionaire and the founder of Standard Oil, which became one of the most powerful monopolies in United States history. From his earliest days, Rockefeller combined a natural aptitude for numbers with an almost obsessive discipline in managing money. At the age of sixteen, he entered bookkeeping and quickly developed a lifelong habit of meticulously recording every cent earned and spent – a practice he maintained throughout his life.[1]

---

1. Segall, Grant. *John D. Rockefeller: Anointed with Oil*. Oxford University Press, 2001.

Rockefeller's career was defined by his insatiable drive to expand. He reinvested profits with an eye toward efficiency and domination, steadily absorbing competitors until Standard Oil controlled more than 90 percent of the U.S. refining industry. He justified this consolidation as "order out of chaos," but the sheer scale reflected his deeper impulse toward accumulation. Even after amassing fortunes beyond imagination, he pressed for still greater efficiency, larger networks, and wider control. He seemed to have an insatiable drive for more.

While Rockefeller gave generously in later years, endowing universities, medical research, and missions, he was never fully at rest. His quest for "more" was not simply financial but also reputational – he sought more stability, more security, more certainty. The very habits that made him successful also bound him to a cycle of relentless expansion. Rockefeller's story embodies the paradox of wealth: it can create vast institutions for the public good, but it can never in itself identify when it is "enough."

Rockefeller never ceased building, never ceased planning, never ceased seeking more. It is said that when a reporter once asked him, "How much money is enough?" Rockefeller famously replied, "Just a little bit more."

At Rockefeller's peak, his net worth was between an inflation-adjusted amount of $400 billion to $500 billon dollars. He was the early 1900's version of Elon Musk. Yet, with all of that wealth, power and influence, he still didn't feel like it was enough.

If someone with the wealth of Rockefeller wasn't satisfied with his material assets, it begs the question, "Is there ever an end to the human desire for more?" The answer based on the evidence at hand is a resounding "no!", yet we still fall prey to the myth of more.

This isn't a modern-day phenomenon, or something brought about by the industrial revolution. This desire for more has been around as long as humans have been on this planet.

In fact, Jesus addresses this issue in his day by telling a particular story about a man who had his focus on "more."

※

One day, when teaching a large crowd, a man shouts out to Jesus, "... tell my brother to divide the inheritance with me." Jesus declines to do so but takes the opportunity to make a teaching point to the crowd:

> "Take care, and be on your guard against all covetousness,
> for one's life does not consist in the abundance of his
> possessions." Luke 12:15

Let's spend a few minutes dissecting this verse in Greek. The phrase "Take care, and be on guard" is the Greek phrase *Horate kai phylassesthe,* which means "discern clearly and be on guard". It is the image of one who is diligent about recognizing and correctly interpreting the situation at hand. In this verse, Jesus instructs them to take this posture in relation to "all covetousness", or *pases pleonexias. Pleonexias* is a noun derived from *pleion,* meaning "numerically more", and *exo* - "to have". This word literally means "to have more."

Jesus specifically warns the crowd that it is important to be able to rightly discern and guard against any situation where they feel that they must *have more.* Why? Jesus provides the reason for this instruction in the second half of the verse: "...for one's life does not consist in the abundance of his possessions." There are three Greek words that get translated into our English word "life": *bios, psuche,* and *zoe.*

Bios refers to biological life and the things that sustain it, such as: food, wealth, or physical resources. *Psuche* represents the soul-life and is often translated also as "soul". It encompasses the unseen things that are parts of us such as our will, mind and the force that animates our physical body. *Zoe* is considered the highest form of life that is divine or spiritual in nature. You might say "the life that really is life."

Zoe is the word used in Luke 12:15.

"Abundance" is the Greek word *perissueo,* meaning to "super-abound" or "beyond expectation in every way." Not just *more*, but a *whole lot more... more than you dreamed of.*

Putting both halves together, this verse could be rendered: "You must be discerning, carefully guarding against the idea that you need just a little more; for the life that you are really seeking is not found in having more of the things that you can purchase and possess, even much more than you have today."

Where then is the life I am really seeking found?

※

What is the "good life"? How would you define it?

There was a time in my life when I would have defined that as owning my own home and not living paycheck to paycheck. However, once I obtained those things, my definition of the good life also shifted. It became about developing a savings account, building a retirement fund, and working towards freedom from financial stressors. After those things were in place with a process to grow them, then the line moved again and became about upgrades: bigger/nicer house in a better neighborhood, a newer/nicer car, and other technology (tv, phone, computer, etc.). Somewhere along the way, career success and recognition became very important, along with physical health. Finally, I longed for personal freedom and autonomy – zero constraints. I called this "living life on my terms." I wanted to say, along with Frank Sinatra at the end of it all, "I did it my way."

The issue I discovered is that there was always more. More that can be done. More than can be achieved. More to want. It's funny about that word "more." It doesn't matter where you start on the treadmill of life – there is *always* more.

The greatest problem with "more" is that it never arrives. The moment we gain what we longed for, the target shifts. A new house becomes too small, a promotion quickly feels inadequate, and yesterday's luxuries turn into today's expectations. "More" keeps whispering, Just a little further. Just one step higher. Then you'll be satisfied. But the promise is hollow. Like a mirage, "more" recedes the closer we get to it.

Our culture intensifies this illusion. From billboards to Instagram ads, we are constantly reminded of what we lack and who we could be – *If only we had more.*

At this point in the biblical story, Jesus doesn't stop with a warning. He tells a parable to show just how deceptive "more" really is:

> "The land of a rich man produced plentifully, and he thought to himself, 'What shall I do, for I have nowhere to store my crops?' And he said, 'I will do this: I will tear down my barns and build larger ones, and there I will store all my grain and my goods. And I will say to my soul, 'Soul, you have ample goods laid up for many years; relax, eat, drink, be merry.' (Luke 12:16–19)

While this story clearly had application in the 1st century A.D., does it no also resonate with you and I? Isn't this the picture of someone who is the epitome of what many of us in America are spending our lives pursuing? Finally achieving financial independence with a large retirement nest egg that will last him the rest of his days on earth, he sits back to enjoy the fruits for which he has been laboring his whole life.

What is the one word God uses to describe someone who lives such a life?

> But God said to him, 'Fool! This night your soul is required of you, and the things you have prepared, whose will they be?' So is the one who lays up treasure for himself and is not rich toward God." (Luke 12:20-21

Fool.

This is the Greek word *aphron*. It is a combination of *a (without)* and *phren (inner perspective that regulates behavior)*. You and I might use "fool" in a number of ways, but here the word means a person who lacks perspective because they are short-sighted – they are not seeing the overall picture that is needed to act wisely.

The rich man's problem in Jesus' parable wasn't his success. The issue was his assumption that "more" equaled the "good life." Notice the language of accumulation: my crops... my barns... my grain... my goods... my soul. His world. His needs. His desires. It was a life built on self. He was the center of his own universe. He lived Sinatra's song... he did it his way. How many of us consider this man's sentiments and success the core of what we call "The American Dream"? Is this not the illusion that so many of us are chasing? We may not admit it in so many words, but do not our actions, calendar and bank accounts supply all of the evidence that would be needed for a judge to declare "guilty!" in a court of law?

"Fool." This is the divine verdict on a life lived this way. A life spent stockpiling "more." The man in the story confused that abundance with significance. His barns were full, but his soul was empty. He was rich in assets but bankrupt before God.

Jesus' parable brings us face to face with the critical question: What are we living for? Are we chasing "just a little more," or are we pursuing the kind of life that truly satisfies... the life that is only found in God Himself?

This story echoes Rockefeller's restless pursuit of "just a little bit more." The rich man had plenty, but he convinced himself that what he needed was bigger barns – more storage, more security, more cushion for the future. His vision of the "good life" was simple: relax, eat, drink, and enjoy. Yet God interrupts that dream with the ultimate reality check: *life itself is not in his control*. His barns could not keep him alive one hour longer.

We can make more money – we cannot make *more time*. And you and I do no know how much of it we have left. So far the statistics hold up pretty well to the most severe scrutiny: 1 out of 1 people die. The odds are 100%. The fix is in. It is a sure thing. The parable ends just as abruptly as some lives do: "This night your soul is required of you."

No long moral, no softened landing. Just the reality that life is fleeting and possessions cannot save. Jesus leaves us with a haunting truth... our barns will crumble, but our souls will stand before God.

And that is where the story presses on us. If Rockefeller, with all his billions, still wanted more, what makes us think our hearts will be satisfied with just a little extra? If the man in Jesus' parable could not secure his life with bigger barns, what makes us believe our bigger houses, fuller calendars, or padded accounts will do any better?

The question is not really whether we will pursue treasure... it's *where*.

What "barn" am I building to feel safe, important, or fulfilled?
Where do I believe "more" will finally be enough?

The hard, hallow truth is that everything you own will one day end up in the landfill. Every. Single. Thing.

However, your soul will live on.

Considering that, how are you choosing to live your one and only life?

"You cannot serve both God and money." (Matthew 6:24)

That verse is not about how much you have and it's not about how well you budget. This Greek root word for "serve" is *doulos* and it means "slave." This is about what you are ordering your life around. What is at the center? Whatever is at the center of your life is the primary source of your security, identity, purpose and meaning. It is the thing that you are willing to make sacrifices for, the thing that dictates your decisions, and the thing that justifies your actions.

Jesus here is saying that can be God or that can be material wealth, but it cannot be both. You cannot follow Jesus while at the same time have a plan to strike it rich. In our minds we think we can hold those two things in tension and pursue both, but those ideas are at odds with each other. They cannot cohabitate in the same heart, because *they both demand to be God*.

There is only one throne in your heart, and only one can occupy it.

The question is, which one will you choose?

CHAPTER TEN

CROSS MY HEART AND HOPE TO DIE

"WHEN THEY HAD FINISHED BREAKFAST, JESUS SAID TO SIMON PETER, 'SIMON, SON OF JOHN, DO YOU LOVE ME MORE THAN THESE?'" JOHN 21:15

W hen I was between the ages of 2 and 5 years old, my family lived in a trailer park in Fayetteville, Georgia. My earliest memories originate there, with a few that really stand out. One of those times was the day I helped a friend destroy a toy out of sheer curiosity. In 1976, a large gel-filled action figure was first sold by the toy maker Kenner. It was the image of a shirtless muscleman with blonde hair and black shorts. The figure was known as "Stretch Armstrong."

"Stretch" was an apropos moniker because the guy, with enough effort from you and a friend, could be pulled from his original 15" in height to nearly 5 feet in length. Stretch's skin felt like it was made of rubber, but the real question that often came up in our kid-conversations was "What's inside?" It was amazing to see this toy maintain its elasticity – you could stretch him out as far as you could pull him, and then eventually he would return to his original size. It wasn't instantaneous. The more you stretched him, the longer it took him to return to his normal size, but he always eventually did.

What was this magic that allowed for Stretch to accomplish this feat? It felt like some great secret of the universe.

I didn't have a Stretch of my own, but one of my friends who lived in the trailer behind ours did. When we were at his place one day, curiosity got the better of both of us, and we decided we simply had to know what was inside. We pulled and tugged with everything we had on a leg, then an arm, but no matter how much force we applied, we couldn't seem to get the skin to tear. After about 20 minutes of frustration, my friend decided to get his mom's scissors from her sewing kit. He left the room for a few seconds while I got nervous with excitement that we might be the first kids to ever see what was contained inside. We were going to be the kid version of Neil Armstrong – one small cut for kiddom, one giant leap for kid-kind.

When my friend came back with the scissors, our eyes locked for a moment like doctors about to perform a radical surgery. Then he took Stretch's left leg and cut into it. To my surprise, nothing immediately came out. I was expecting a burst of something – some gel, some plasma, some ooze... but nothing. My friend took the leg, pulled it, and twisted it. It was then that we saw a clear, thick substance start to slide out of the opening he had made with his scissors. It seemed like really thick and sticky jelly. That's it. It was very anticlimactic. The biggest issue was that now Stretch's leg wasn't shrinking back to its original size. His left leg was about twice as long as his other leg, and even though we tried to push and shape it back to its original form, that wasn't happening. I saw the fear on my friend's face when he had the future vision of his parents finding out about the surgery we had just performed. He quickly grabbed Stretch and threw him in the corner of his closet and then buried him under a pile of other toys and dolls he and his sister shared. My friend then looked at me and said, "Promise me you'll NEVER tell anyone! Promise!!"

"I won't!" I cried, and followed it up with "Cross my heart and hope to die!" I backed up my word by pledging my 4-year-old life. Solid as a rock.

A few days later, when my friend's mom had found the mutilated Stretch at the bottom of my friend's closet, she called my mom to inquire if I knew what had happened. Under threat of notifying my father when he got home from work, I sang like a jaybird. Not only did I tell my mom what my friend had done to Stretch, but that I was pleading against it the whole time. I shared how I had done my best to stop my friend's murderous intentions, to no avail. I knew my mom didn't believe me, but she overlooked my personal culpability in exchange for the truth that Stretch's leg had been cut open with scissors to expose what was inside his body.

Sometimes the vows we make in the moment aren't strong enough to bear up under the weight of the consequences. I had made a rash vow to Timmy. While my story is a light-hearted reminiscence, there are other examples we all have of violating a vow we made that are much more serious, with consequences that are more grave.

The focus of this chapter is on a vow the disciple Peter made, then broke; but even more so about Jesus' profound response to that betrayal that holds out hope for us all.

Every.

Single.

One.

❈

Before we get to the vow that Peter breaks, we need to complete a brief biographical sketch of what we know about Peter and some inferences that are safe to draw.

Peter is originally from Bethsaida (John 1:44), which was a village situated on the northeastern shore of the Sea of Galilee. Bethsaida means "house of fishing" (Hebrew: *Beit-Tsaida; Beit* = "house" and *Taisda* = fishing/hunting), therefore it is no surprise the Peter's occupation is that of a fisherman (Mark 1:16). We can also infer that Peter doesn't just have a job, it is a business venture for him because we are told he owns his own boat and is in partnership in the business with James and John, all three of which become disciples of Jesus (Luke 5:1-11). Eventually, Peter makes his home in Capernaum (Mark 1:29), which is on the northwest shore of the Sea, about 6 miles from Bethsaida "as the crow flies." Capernaum was a larger trade hub located on the Via Maris (major ancient thoroughfare) and would have been a better location for Peter's fishing business.

What about Peter's age? This is a significant aspect of the disciples in general that has been overlooked by modern society. I think most of us have the image of the disciples being middle-aged men with 5 o'clock shadows, primarily because that is how they are so often portrayed by media. Even in a modern-day series like *The Chosen* that attempts to give us an accurate picture of what it might have been like back then, the disciples are all grown men. It is highly likely that the disciples are not only younger than we think, but *much younger*. Would it shock you to know that scripture shows us that Peter was the only disciple over 20 years old? We see evidence of their age in Matthew 17:24-27. We are told that when the disciples and Jesus arrive in Capernaum, the "collectors of the two-drachma tax" approach Peter and ask if Jesus pays this tax. There is a tax that is commanded in Exodus 30:14 that every male over the age of 20 would pay for the upkeep of the temple. Peter told those collecting the tax that it was Jesus' custom to pay it, and presumably went in the house to notify Jesus of the situation; however Jesus sees him and speaks first:

> "... go to the lake and throw out your line. Take the first fish you catch; open its mouth and you will find a four-drachma coin. Take it and give it to them for my tax and yours." Matthew 17:27

We have already been told that all of the disciples are there. Why does Jesus command this miracle fish to only produce a four-drachma coin if its a two-drachma tax per person? Because Jesus and Peter are *the only two males of the crew who are 20 years old or over.*

This means that the rest of the disciples are teenagers. This event happens nearing the end of Jesus' three year ministry – so outside of Peter, the oldest the disciples could have possibly been when they started to follow Jesus was *16 years old.* Chances are good that several of them were younger, perhaps as young as 13.

It is quite natural that the younger disciples would have looked up to Peter as their leader.

While he was a fisherman (for fish anyway) he was not known as Peter, since that was not his actual name. Peter is a nickname that Jesus gave him (John 1:42), but his mother gave him the name Simon

– or *Shim'on* in Hebrew. The name comes from the Hebrew root word *shema,* which means "hear" or "listen". So *Shim'on* means "he has heard". This name holds significant spiritual meaning. What is widely considered the most important prayer in Judaism is called the Shema and comes from the beginning verse of the prayer *Shema yisrael, adonai eloheinu, adonai echad* – "Hear O Israel, the LORD is our God, the LORD alone." (Deuteronomy 6:4) As you might recall me describing biblical Hebrew words as "overstuffed suitcases", the word *shema* means not just to audibly hear something, but carries with it the additional action of obedience. It means to listen with the intention to obey.

In the Hebrew way of thinking, a person's name was not just something the parents gave them because they thought it sounded good. The name to a Hebrew gives identity and even confers destiny. The root of Simon's name is all about obedient action, and we see in the scriptures that Peter is all about action. Peter is typically the first to take charge in situations with the disciples, he gets out of the boat in the storm to walk on water, he speaks up to ask Jesus to explain the parables, he is the first to declare that Jesus is the Messiah, he has the audacity to rebuke Jesus at one point, and at Jesus' arrest he draws his sword and cuts off the ear of the servant of the high priest. Simon is decisive, impulsive, and occasionally looking for a fight.

One last thing that is unique to Simon. Jesus gives him the name Peter the first time he meets him, and then reiterates it again in Matthew 16:

"And Jesus answered him, 'Blessed are you, Simon son of Jonah! For flesh and blood has not revealed this to you, but my Father who is in heaven. And I tell you, you are Peter, and on this rock I will build my church.'" Matthew 16:17-18

The name Peter means "rock". In the Bible, it is a pretty big deal when God changes a person's name. He changes Abram to Abraham, Sarai to Sarah, Jacob to Israel, Hoshea to Joshua, and Saul to Paul. This is very elite company Simon Peter has just found himself in. I imagine Peter must have held his chest out at least a little more when God incarnate tells you, "you are a rock... and one that I will build my church on!"

Peter. The Oldest. One of the first called. A man of action. A man whom God renames. The leader of the disciples.

The higher you climb, the harder you fall. And Peter takes a fall. A hard one.

●

That fall began on the night of Jesus' arrest.

The disciples had just shared the Passover meal with their Lord in the upper room. Jesus had washed their feet, broken the bread, and passed the cup. He then told them plainly that one of them would betray Him. After three years of incredible teaching, the witness of miracles, and the love that would have developed between Jesus and his closest companions, this revelation must have been seen as hardly believable. But Peter, likely prompted by incredulity and the desire to be the example for his younger brothers, in true Peter fashion, takes a stand:

"Even if all fall away on account of you, I never will." (Matt. 26:33)

I have no doubt in my heart that Peter actually believed what he said. I do not think Peter could envision a scenario where he would turn and betray his love and fidelity to his Lord.

During this episode in Luke, we read Jesus providing Peter with a profound warning:

> "Simon, Simon, Satan has asked to sift all of you as wheat. But I have prayed for you, Simon, that your faith may not fail. And when you have turned back, strengthen your brothers." (Luke 22:31–32)

Notice that Jesus calls Peter "Simon" in these verses – not just once, but three times in a very short span. Why is Jesus doing that? "Simon" is who he was before he came to know Jesus. Why refer back to that name now?

Secondarily, but just as important, Jesus says "...when you have turned back..." Jesus is clearly telling him that *he will fall away*, and after a period of time, he will come back – but not only that, Jesus *tells him what to do when he returns:* "... strengthen your brothers."

Do not miss this fact: even before Peter stumbled, *Jesus was already past it.* Jesus was busy planning for what would need to happen after Peter's repentance *from a sin he had yet to even commit.*

He was in effect saying to Peter – "Look you are going to mess it up pretty bad, but once you have repented – once you have returned – your brothers will need you."

Next, Peter doubles down and stakes his pledge on his very life.

> "Peter said to him, 'Lord, I am ready to go with you both to prison and to death.' Jesus said, 'I tell you, Peter, the rooster will not crow this day, until you deny three times that you know me.'" Luke 22:33

"Even if I have to die with you, I will never disown you."
(Matt. 26:35)

Cross his heart and hope to die.

Did you notice that Jesus now addresses him as "Peter" in Luke 22:33? That's interesting. He just called him "Simon" three times, why switch back? There are not two individuals here Jesus is speaking to, but are there two people? There is Simon. Then there is Peter. They just exist in one package. There is the Simon that he was before he came to know Jesus... and now the Peter that he has become.

Perhaps the question is: Which one will he be tonight?

Peter's words were sincere, but sincerity is not the same as strength. A vow made in the heat of the moment may not have the endurance to survive the cold night of testing.

And it didn't.

In Gethsemane, when the soldiers arrived, Peter acted on impulse. He drew his sword and cut off the ear of the high priest's servant (John 18:10). It was vintage Peter. Decisive, bold, and reckless. But Jesus rebuked him and healed the man.

Then came the courtyard. Jesus was inside, on trial before the high priest. Peter warmed himself by the fire outside. A servant girl asked, "You also were with Jesus of Galilee, weren't you?" (John 18:17) Peter denied it.

Another voice accused him. Again, Peter denied it. (John 18:25)

A third time, someone insisted, "Surely you are one of them, your accent gives you away." Then Peter began to call down curses, swearing he never knew Jesus. (Mark 14:71)

And the rooster crowed.

Luke adds a haunting detail: "The Lord turned and looked straight at Peter." (Luke 22:61)

Can you imagine that moment? The Rock... the leader... the one who pledged his very life only a few short hours ago... caught in the gaze of the One he had just denied... repeatedly... with curses. Peter ran out and "wept bitterly." (Luke 22:62) The phrase "wept bitterly" is the Greek *klaio pikros*. It has the connotation of violence, and transliterated as "wailed violently."

Three years of walking with Jesus, of witnessing miracles, of seeing the kingdom come in action, of taking a leadership role amongst the disciples, of being the "rock" God was supposed to build his church on... all undone in a single night.

Jesus is tried, convicted, crucified, and buried. Seemingly the end of the story.

Then on the first day of the week, something happens. Surely Peter had two of the most fitful, sleepless nights of his life when Mary Magdalene found Peter and John and told them that someone had stolen the body of Jesus from the tomb. They ran to the tomb and indeed found it empty. They also saw something strange: they "... saw the linen cloths lying there and the face cloth, which had been on Jesus' head, not lying with the linen cloths, but folded up in a place by itself." (John 20:6-7) The body is gone, but the grave clothes are still there. Why would someone unwrap his body and take it? They do not know what has happened, but according to John the resurrection was not a part of their thinking for we read "for as yet they did not understand the scripture, that he must rise from the dead." (John 20:10)

Then things really get strange as Jesus began to appear to the disciples, and if first they think they are seeing an apparition. It is only after several encounters that they understand what has actually happened. Jesus has resurrected from the dead.

Imagine how unbelievable... how incredible... how amazing all of this would have been to the disciples. How many questions they must have had! How confused they must have been. Scripture even shares that for 40 days after the resurrection, Jesus was seen by more than 500 people, interacting and teaching them. Yet on the day he would ascend back to heaven, we read, "And when they saw him they worshiped him, but some doubted." Even still they had reservations.

Taking all of that in, let's consider that Peter is not only feeling all of that, but also the weight of his complete denial of Jesus to save his own skin. We are still many days away from the powerful Peter who preaches on Pentecost, and as a result, 3,000 people are saved. This Peter isn't considering ministry. He is going back to his life before Jesus.

We read in John chapter 21 that Peter, Thomas, James, John and two other disciples are hanging out one day and then Peter speaks up:

> "Simon Peter said to them, 'I am going fishing.' They said to him, 'We will go with you.' They went out and got into the boat, but that night they caught nothing." John 21:3

Another night of futility. What a way to get back into the family business.

> "Just as day was breaking, Jesus stood on the shore; yet the disciples did not know that it was Jesus. Jesus said to them, 'Children, do you have any fish?'" John 21:4-5a

At that moment, though they didn't recognize the man standing on the shore, a part of me wonders – did they hear something familiar in the voice? Something familiar in what he said? Did Peter recall the first time he encountered Jesus when he was fishing – after another fruitless night?

> "And when he (Jesus) had finished speaking, he said to Simon, "Put out into the deep and let down your nets for a catch.' And Simon answered, 'Master, we toiled all night and took nothing! But at your word I will let down the nets.'" Luke 5:4-5

In that moment, the nets were so full the boats began to sink...

Or did they recall the times they did have a few small fish, and witnessed thousands of people being fed by the miracle their master performed?

Chills must have run up their spines when the stranger on the shore then said:

> "He said to them, 'Cast the net on the right side of the boat, and you will find some'. John 21:6a

Could it be?

> "So they cast it, and now they were not able to haul it in, because of the quantity of fish." John 21:6b

The word tells us "When Simon Peter heard that it was the Lord, he... threw himself into the sea." Peter had stepped out of a boat once before to go to Jesus – this time he *throws himself* into the sea in a rush to get to his Lord.

After breakfast and a happy reunion, Jesus pulls Peter aside to address the elephant on the shore:

> "When they had finished breakfast, Jesus said to Simon
> Peter, 'Simon, son of John, do you love me more than
> these?' He said to him, 'Yes, Lord; you know that I love
> you.' He said to him, 'Feed my lambs'. He said to him a
> second time, 'Simon, son of John, do you love me?' He
> said to him, 'Yes, Lord; you know that I love you.' He said
> to him, 'Tend my sheep.' He said to him the third time,
> 'Simon, son of John, do you love me?' Peter was grieved
> because he said to him the third time, 'Do you love me?'
> and he said to him, 'Lord, you know everything; you know
> that I love you.' Jesus said to him, 'Feed my sheep.'" John
> 21:15-18

In a beautifully symmetrical fashion, Jesus offers Simon three opportunities to declare his fidelity to Jesus – one for each denial.

As Peter declares in those verses, Jesus knows everything. Jesus already knew Peter loved him... why the questions? Because Peter needed it. Something inside his humanity needed to vocalize his repentant love for his Lord. For himself. So his wounded heart could heal.

There is something very instructive for you and I in this story.

Before the rooster ever crowed, Christ had already written the next chapter of Peter's story. While Peter thought his failure disqualified him,

Jesus had already moved beyond it. That is the breathtaking reality of a God who stands outside of time. He sees both our collapse and our restoration in the same moment. We sit in guilt and regret, but He sits in sovereign grace, waiting at the shore.

Jesus not only offered Peter forgiveness; He gave him an assignment. Each question of love was matched with a command: "Feed my sheep." In the same way, our failures do not end our calling – they deepen it.

Peter's story reminds us that God does not leave us imprisoned in our failures. While Peter was drowning in regret, Jesus had already moved beyond the denials and prepared a place for repentance. The risen Lord did not simply absolve Peter; He restored him.

It is the same for us. While we often replay our sins in endless guilt, the Lord is already waiting on the shore, ready to welcome us back and send us forward. Repentance is never the end of our story, but the beginning of a renewed mission.

After your rooster has crowed, you can still be restored to lead.

Restored to serve.

Restored to love.

EPILOGUE: THE QUESTIONS THAT REMAIN

L et's have a brief, intimate conversation. You and me.

Not the "generic you" reading this book. The specific you.

For all of the reasons a person might reject the American Christian church (there are many) and the Jesus it claims to represent, one thing remains true:

"For the Son of Man came to seek and to save the lost." (Luke 19:10)

It was the entire reason Jesus came to this earth. To seek you and to save you. You. You may read that and say "I don't need saving." If you feel that way, my guess is because we in the church have done a pretty good job of telling you that you are a sinner, destined for eternal torment because there is nothing good in you. The only way for you to be saved from this outcome – ultimately saved from God Himself – is to believe that Jesus was God, lived a perfect life, died the death you deserved, and offers you the free gift of not going to hell when your days living in this body are over. It's a great escape plan. Makes the choice really simple – if you don't want to burn endlessly for eternity, then pray this prayer. You can make me "believe" all sorts of things if the only other alternative is the damnation of my soul. Sort of a "In case of emergency, break glass" message. It is the message I heard repeatedly growing up in the churches I attended.

You could also make me really "want" to give you my wallet if you put a gun to my ribs. Fear can make us "want" to do lots of things. Is this motivation the one God had in mind... fear?

"Anyone who does not love does not know God, because God is love." (1 John 4:8)

God *is* love. Love is *not an aspect* of His nature. *He is love itself.*

Does Love then traffic in fear? Is fear the tool that Love itself uses to achieve its purpose?

"There is no fear in love, but perfect love casts out fear. For fear has to do with punishment, and whoever fears has not been perfected in love." (1 John 4:18)

Let me be clear, in case its not obvious, I have yet to die. I know (meaning knowing by experience) as much as you do about death (unless you have died). Do the scriptures speak of a place called hell that seems to be a location that some souls wind up that is apart from the presence of God? Yes. I say "seems" because well-meaning, highly educated people differ widely on how those verses should be interpreted. I'm not arguing for or against any one position here.

I'm asking the question – is an appeal designed to scare you into heaven someday the best God can do? Is it the best *love* can do? Or is it simply the most effective argument we humans have developed to gain converts?

Let's return to why Jesus himself says that he came. We will dissect the "seek and to save" verse in a moment. First a few more verses from Jesus himself about his purpose:

"For God did not send his Son into the world to condemn the world, but in order that the world might be saved through him." (John 3:17)

"For I did not come to judge the world but to save the world." (John 12:47)

"I came that they may have life and have it abundantly." (John 10:10)

"I came into the world as light, so that whoever believes in me may not remain in darkness." (John 12:46)

It's worth noting Jesus doesn't seem to be talking about taking people to heaven in these verses. He seems to be talking about life here, now, on this earth.

You might ask, "Well, what about these references to 'saving the world? Isn't that about going to heaven?" This hinges on what you believe the word "save" to mean. For many of us, the word "save" is synonymous with idea of getting my ticket to heaven when I die, as opposed to hell. Saved *from* hell. Saved from being another piece of kindling on the fire.

But is that what this word translated as "save" means?

The Greek root word translated as "save" in these verses (and in most of the others) is *sozo*. It has less to do with getting out of here someday (as you and I define it today) and much more to do with healing and wholeness now. In fact, when not translated as "save" it is mostly translated as "made well" or "made whole." There are other Greek words that carry more of the theology of salvation when it comes to redemption, ransom, and rescue, but they are not *sozo*.

What if we rendered these verses, "For God did not send his Son into the world to condemn the world, but in order that the world might be healed through him?" Or, "For I did not come to judge the world but to make the world whole?"

Could our world use some healing? Some wholeness?

What about you? Could *your* world use some of that?

What if the good news is that Jesus came to seek us out and save us from our brokenness individually and collectively – to heal us, and make us whole – here, now, on this earth? And what if that relationship of healing and wholeness with God is an eternal one? When our bodies finally give out, our spirit continues on to live in the presence of the One who sought us in the first place? That this God who is seeking me, is not just interested in what happens after I die, but interested in moving me towards healing and wholeness now. In my heart and in my relationships. What if part of the good news is that not only is God interested in those things for my own life, but I also get to be an agent of bringing His health, healing and wholeness into the world I live in?

Now *that* would be good news. That would actually be *great* news. Doesn't participation in *that* plan sound a lot better than "if you don't make this choice, you'll burn?"

That is what Jesus means here by "save".

So what about seeking? If God is seeking me, and its why Jesus came... then how does that happen, and what does it feel like when it is happening?

First the "how." There are parables in the Bible that talk about God's seeking heart. The shepherd who leaves the 99 sheep to go find the 1 who is lost. The woman who overturns her entire house to find the coin she has lost. While I agree that these parables reflect God's heart in seeking us, they do not accurately reflect how that happens. God is all-knowing. He doesn't have to shake out the couch cushions to find you. He isn't roaming through the night looking for you. He already knows exactly where you are at each hour of the day in every way, physically, emotionally and spiritually. So then how does God seek?

"For the Son of Man came to seek and to save the lost."

The Greek word for seek in this verse is the root word *zeteo*. It means to seek by *inquiring*. What is the action you undertake when you are inquiring? Asking questions.

God seeks you by asking questions.

How, then, do you know when God is seeking you? It's often in the quiet spaces, when it's just you and the truth and a question rises up from the depths of your soul: "Where are you?" "What are you doing here?" "Do you want to be healed?" "Do you love me?" "Why do you feel like you were meant for more than this?" "You have so much, why are you not satisfied or content?"

These questions that bubble up are not just questions from a psyche dealing with existential angst, but rather evidence of the curious nature of a God who asks questions. Questions He is depositing in your soul. It's one of His primary ways of seeking you. To cause you to seek Him. For what purpose? To heal you. To make you whole. Not in an instant, not overnight, but in a process that starts here and now. In a relationship that truly will last forever.

The last question from me is... how will you respond?

It is 9:34 a.m. Central Daylight Time on August 30th, 2025. I have just completed the final chapter of this book – my first.

Thank you for coming along on this journey with me. I am so grateful that you decided to pick up this book and that you found enough value to make it all the way to the end.

My hope is that, as you've walked through these pages, you've gained a new appreciation for what God's questions reveal – not just about the people in Scripture, but about you, about me, and about His enduring, patient, and unfailing love. Even when we fail, even when we stumble, He is already beyond it, waiting for us to return, ready to restore, ready to set us back on the path He has for us.

Because the story God wants us to be telling is not the one of failure, but of restoration. Every. Single. Time.

Now, as one of my great spiritual mentors would say:

Grace and Peace, my friends.

-BD

P.S. – If you'd like to stay connected, you can find me on all social media, or drop me a line at questionsgodasks.com Let's connect!

CONTRIBUTORS

I could not have written this book without the review and insight of some pretty special people. Here they are in no particular order:

Maureen Schein, Austin Lane, Chris Wammack, Darin Teague, Debbie Teague, Esther George, David McVicker, Jennifer Langan, Scott Langan, Joe Cella, John Martin, Joyce Ross, Lesa Parry, Rob Parry, Richard Salinas, Stephanie Valdez, Virginia Guevara, Tom Yager, Dan Williams, Margie Pfeiler, Chuck Dunham, Naomi Dunham, and Chris Dunham.

If it takes a village to write a book, you are all residents!

APPENDIX

ALL THE QUESTIONS GOD ASKS

1. Gen 3:9 – "The LORD God called out to the man, 'Where are you?'"

2. Gen 3:11 – "He said, 'Who told you that you were naked? Have you eaten of the tree which I commanded of you not to eat?"

3. Gen 3:13 – "The the LORD God said to the woman, 'What is this that you have done?'

4. Gen 4:6 – "The LORD said to Cain, 'Why are you angry, and why has your face fallen?'"

5. Gen 4:7 – "If you do well, will you not be accepted?"

6. Gen 4:9 – "Then the LORD said to Cain, 'Where is Able your brother?'"

7. Gen 4:10 – "And the LORD said, "What have you done?"

8. Gen 16:8 – "And he said, 'Hagar, servant of Sarai, where have you come from and where are you going?"

9. Gen 18:9 – "They said to him, 'Where is Sarah your wife?'"

10. Gen 18:13 – "The LORD said to Abraham, 'Why did Sarah laugh and say, 'Shall I indeed bear a child now that I am old?''"

11. Genesis 18:14 – "Is anything too hard for the LORD?"

12. Genesis 18:17 – "The LORD said, 'Shall I hide from Abraham what I am about to do, seeing that Abraham shall surely become a great

and mighty nation, and all the nations of the earth shall be blessed in him?'"

13. Genesis 19:12 – "Then the men said to Lot 'Have you anyone else here?..'"

14. Gen 21:17 – "And God heard the voice of the boy, and the agnel of God called to Hagar from heaven and said to her, 'What troubles you, Hagar?..'"

15. Gen 32:29 – "...But he said, 'Why is it that you ask my name?'"

16. Exodus 4:2 – "The LORD said to him, 'What is that in your hand?'"

17. Exodus 4;11 – "Then the LORD said to him, 'Who has made man's mouth?'"

18. Exodus 4:11 – "...Who makes him mute, or deaf, or seeing, or blind?"

19. Exodus 4:11 – "Is it not I the LORD?"

20. Exodus 4:14 – "...is there not Aaron, your brother, the Levite?"

21. Exodus 14:15 – "Then the LORD said to Moses, 'Why do you cry to me?'"

22. Numbers 11:23 – "And the LORD said to Moses, 'Is the LORD's hand shortened?'"

23. Numbers 12:8 –"...why then were you not afraid to speak against my servant Moses?"

24. Numbers 14:11 – "And the LORD said to Moses, 'How long will this people despise me?"

25. Numbers 14:11 – "...and how long will they not believe in me, in spite of all the signs that I have done among them?"

26. Numbers 14:27 – "How long shall this wicked congregation grumble against me?"

27. Numbers 22:9 – "And God came to Balaam and said, 'Who are these men with you?'"

28. Numbers 22:32 – "And the angel of the LORD said to him , "Why have you struck your donkey these three times?"

29. Joshua 1:9 – "Have I not commanded you?"

30. Joshua 7:10 – "The LORD said to Joshua, 'Get up! Why have you fallen on your face?'"

31. Judges 2:2 – "...what is this that you have done?" *

32. Judges 6:14 – "And the LORD turned to him and said, 'Go in this might of yours and save Israel from the hand of Midian; did not I send you?'"

33. Judges 10:11 – "And the LORD said to the people of Israel, 'Did I not save you from the Egyptians and from the Amorites, from the Ammonites and from the Philistines?'"

34. Judges 13:18 – "And the angel of the LORD said to him, "Why do you ask my name, seeing it is wonderful?'"

35. 1 Sam 16:1 – "The LORD said to Samuel, 'How long will you grieve over Saul, since I have rejected him from being king over Israel?'"

36. 2 Sam 7:5 – "Go and tell my servant David, 'Thus says the Lord: Would you build me a house to dwell in?'"

37. 2 Sam 7:7 – "In all the places where I have moved with all the people of Israel, did I speak a word with any of the judges of Israel, whom I commanded to shepherd my people Israel, saying 'Why have you not built me a house of cedar?'

38. 2 Sam 12:9 – "Why have you despised the word of the LORD, to do what is evil in his sight?"

39. 1 Kings 19:9 – "There he came to a cave and lodged in it. And behold, the word of the LORD came to him, and he said to him, 'What are you doing here, Elijah?'"

40. 1 Kings 19:13 – "And when Elijah heard it he wrapped his face in his cloak and went out and stood at the entrance to the cave. And behold, there came a voice to him and said, 'What are you doing here Elijah?'"

41. 1 Kings 20:13 – "And behold, a prophet came near to Ahab king of Israel and said, "Thus says the LORD, Have you seen all this great multitude?...'"

42. 1 Kings 21:19 – "And you shall say to him 'Thus says the LORD, 'Have you killed and also taken possession?'"

43. 1 Kings 21:29 – "Have you seen how Ahab has humbled himself before me?"

44. 2 Kings 1:3 – "But the angel of the LORD said to Elijah the Tishbite, 'Arise, go up to meet the messengers of the king of Samaria, and say to them, 'Is it because there is no God in Israel that you are going to inquire of Baal-zebub, the god of Ekron?'"

45. 2 Kings 1:16 – "...and said to him, 'Thus says the LORD, 'Because you have sent messengers to inquire of Baal-zebub, the god of Ekron - is it because there is no God in Israel to inquire of his word?'"

46. 2 Kings 19:22 – "Whom have you mocked and reviled?"

47. 2 Kings 19:22 – "Against whom have you raised your voice and lifted your eyes to the heights?"

48. 2 Kings 19:25 – "Have you not heard that I determined it long ago?"

49. 2 Chron 18:19 – "And the LORD said, 'Who will entice Ahab the king of Israel, that he may go up and fall at Ramoth-gilead?'"

50. 2 Chron 18:20 – "Then a spirit came forward and stood before the LORD, saying, 'I will entice him'. And the LORD said to him, 'By what means?'"

51. 2 Chron 24:20 – "...Thus says God, 'Why do you break the commandments of the LORD, so that you cannot prosper?'"

52. 2 Chron 25:15 – "Therefore the LORD was angry with Amaziah and sent to him a prophet, who said to him, 'Why have you sought the gods of a people who did not deliver their own people from your hand?'"

53. Job 1:7 – "The LORD said to Satan, 'From where have you come?'"

54. Job1:8 – "And the LORD said to Satan, 'Have you considered my servant Job, that there is none like him on the earth, a blameless and upright man, who fears God and turns away from evil?'"

55. Job 2:2 – "And the LORD said to Satan, 'From where have you come?'"

56. Job 2:3 – "And the LORD said to Satan, 'Have you considered my servant Job, that there is none like him on the earth, a blameless and upright man, who fears God and turns away from evil?'"

57. Job 38:2 – "Who is this that darkens counsel by words without knowledge?"

58. Job 38:4 – "Where were you when I laid the foundation of the earth?"

59. Job 38:5 – "Who determined its measurements – surely you know!"

60. Job 38:5 – "...Or stretched the line upon it?"

61. Job 38:6-7 – "On what were its bases sunk, or who laid its cornerstone, when the morning stars sang together and all the sons of God shouted for joy?"

62. Job 38:8-11 – "Or who shut in the sea with doors when it burst out from the womb, when I made clouds its garment and thick darkness its swaddling band, and prescribed limits for it and set bars and doors, and said 'Thus far shall you come, and no farther, and here shall you proud waves be stayed?'"

63. Job 38:12-13 – "Have you commanded the morning since your days began, and caused the dawn to know its place, that it might take hold of the skirts of the earth, and the wicked be shaken out of it?"

64. Job 38:16 – "Have you entered into the springs of the sea, or walked in the recesses of the deep?"

65. Job 38:17 – "Have the gates of death been revealed to you, or have you seen the gates of deep darkness?"

66. Job 38:18 – "Have you comprehended the expanse of the earth?"

67. Job 38:19-20 – "Where is the way to the dwelling of light, and where is the place of darkness, that you may take it to its territory and that you may discern the paths to its home?"

68. Job 38:22-23 – "Have you entered the storehouses of the snow, or have you seen the storehouses of the hail, which I have reserved for the time of trouble, for the day of battle and war?"

69. Job 38:24 – "What is the way to theplae wheere thelight is distrib- uted, or where the east wind is scattered upon the earth?"

70. Job 38:25-27 – "Who has cleft a channel for thetorrents of rain and a way for the thunderbolt, to bring rain on a land whereno man is, on he desert in which there is no man, to satisfy the waste anddesolate land, and to make the ground sprout with grass?"

71. Job 38:28 – "Has the rain a father, or who has begotten the drops of dew?"

72. Job 38:29 – "From whose womb did the ice come forth, and who has given birth to the frost of heaven?"

73. Job 38:31 – "Can you bind the chains of the Pleiades or loose the cords or Orion?"

74. Job 38:32 – "Can you lead forth the Mazzaroth intheir season, or can you guide the Bear with its children?"

75. Job 38:33 – "Do you know the ordinances of the heavens?"

76. Job 38:33 – "Can you establish their rule on the earth?"

77. Job 38:34 – "Can you lift up your voice to the clouds, that a flood of waters may cover you?"

78. Job 38:35 – "Can you send forth lightnings that they may go and say to you, 'Here we are'?"

79. Job 38:36 – "Who has put wisdom in the inward parts or given understanding to the mind?"

80. Job 38:37 –"Who can number the clouds by wisdom?"

81. Job 38:37-38 – "Or who can tilt the waterskins of the heavens, when the dust runs into a mass and the clods stick fast together?"

82. Job 38:39-40 – "Can you hunt the prey for the lion, or satisfy the appetite of the young lions, when they crouch in their dens or lie in wait in their thicket?

83. Job 38:41 – "Who provides for the raven its prey, when its young one cry to God for help, and wander about for lack of food?"

84. Job 39:1 – "Do you know when the mountains give birth?"

85. Job 39:1 – "Do you observe the calving of the does?"

86. Job 39:2-3 – "Can you number the months that they fulfill, and do you know the time when they give birth, when they crouch, bring forth their offspring, and are delivered of their young?"

87. Job 39:5 – "Who has let the wild donkey go free?"

88. Job 39:5-6 – "Who has loosed the bonds of the swift donkey, to whom I have given the arid plain for his home and the salt land for his dwelling place?"

89. Job 39:9 – "Is the wild ox willing to serve you?"

90. Job 39:9 – "Will he spend the night at your manger?"

91. Job 39:10 –"Can you bind him in the furrow with ropes, or will he harrow the valleys after you?"

92. Job 39:11 – "Will you depend on him becuase his strength is great, and will you leave to him your labor?"

93. Job 39:12 – "Do you have faith in him that he will return your grain and gather it to your threshing floor?"

94. Job 39:13 – "The wings of the ostrich wave proudly, but are they the pinions and the plumage of love?"

95. Job 39:19 – "Do you give the horse his might?"

96. Job 39:20 – "Do you clothe his neck with a mane?"

97. Job 39:20 – "Do you make him leap like the locust?"

98. Job 39:26 – "Is it by your understanding that the hawk soars and spread his wings toward the south?"

99. Job 39:27 – "Is it at your command that the eagle mounts up and makes his nest on high?"

100. Job 40:2 – "Shall a fault finder contend with the Almighty?"

101. Job 40:8 – "Will you even put me in the wrong?"

102. Job 40:8 – "Will you condemn me that you may be in the right?"

103. Job 40:9 – "Have you an arm like God and can you thunder with a voice like His?"

104. Job 40:24 – "Can one take him by his eyes, or pierce him with a snare?"

105. Job 41:1 – "Can you draw out Leviathan with a fishhook or press down his tongue with a cord?"

106. Job 41:2 – "Can you put a rope in his nose or pierce his jaw with a hook?"

107. Job 41:3 – "Will he make many pleas to you?"

108. Job 41:3 – "Will he speak to you soft words?"

109. Job 41:4 – "Will he make a covenant with you to take him for your servant forever?"

110. Job 41:5 – "Will you play with him as with a bird, or will you put him on a leash for your girls?"

111. Job 41:6 – "Will traders bargain over him?"

112. Job 41:6 – "Will they divide him up among the merchants?"

113. Job 41:7 – "Can you fill his skin with harpoons or his head with fishing spears?"

114. Job 41:10 – "Who then is he who can stand before me?"

115. Job 41:11 – "Who has first given to me, that I should repay him?"

116. Job 41:13 – "Who can strip off his outer garment?"

117. Job 41:13 – "Who would come near him with a bridle?"

118. Job 41:14 – "Who can open the doors of his face?"

119. Psalm 50:13 – "Do I eat the flesh of bulls or drink the blood of goats?"

120. Psalm 50:16 – "But to the wicked God says: 'What right have you to recite my statutes or take my covenant on your lips?'"

121. Isaiah 1:11 – "What to me is the multitude of your sacrifices?" says the LORD

122. Isaiah 1:12 – "When you come to appear before me, ho has required of you this trampling of my courts?"

123. Isaiah 3:15 – "What do you mean by crushing my people, by grinding the face of the poor?"

124. Isaiah 6:8 – "Whom shall I send, and who will go for us?"

125. Isaiah 10:8 – "Are not my commanders all kings?"

126. Isaiah 10:9 – "Is not Calno like Carchemish?"

127. Isaiah 10:9 – "Is not Hamath like Arpad?"

128. Isaiah 10:9 – "Is not Samaria like Damascus?"

129. Isaiah 10:11 – "Shall I not do to Jerusalem and her idols as I have done to Samaria and her images?"

130. Isaiah 22:16 – "What have you to do here, and whom have you here, that you have cut out here a tomb for yourself, you who cut out a tomb on the height and carve a dwelling for yourself in the rock?"

131. Isaiah 28:9 – "To whom will he teach knowledge, and to whom will he explain the message?"

132. Isaiah 28:9 – "Those who are weaned from the milk, those taken from the breast?"

133. Isaiah 40:25 – "To whom then will you compare me, that I should be like him?"

134. Isaiah 40:26 – "Lift up your eyes on high and see: who created these things?"

135. Isaiah 41:4 – "Who has performed and done this, calling the generations from the beginning?"

136. Isaiah 41:26 – "Who declared it from the beginning, that we might know, and before hand, that we might say 'He is right'?"

137. Isaiah 43:13 – "Also henceforth I am he; there is none who can deliver from my hand; I work, and who can turn it back?"

138. Isaiah 43:19 – "Behold I am doing a new thing; now it springs forth, do you not perceive it?"

139. Isaiah 45:9 – "Does the clay say to him who forms it, 'What are you making?'"

140. Isaiah 45:9 – "...or 'Your work has no handles'?"

141. Isaiah 45:11 – "Ask me of things to come; will you command me concerning my children and the work of my hands?"

142. Isaiah 45:21 – "Who told this long ago?"

143. Isaiah 45:21 – "Who declared it of old?"

144. Isaiah 45:21 – "Was it not I, the LORD?"

145. Isaiah 46:5 – "To whom will you liken me and make me equal, and compare me, that we may be alike?"

146. Isaiah 48:6 – "You have heard; now see all this; and will you not declare it?"

147. Isaiah 48:14 – "Assemble all of you and listen! Who among them has declared these things?"

148. Isaiah 49:15 – "Can a woman forget her nursing child, that she should have no compassion on the son of her womb?"

149. Isaiah 50:1 – "Thus says the LORD: 'Where is your mother's certificate of divorce, with which I sent her away?'"

150. Isaiah 50:1 – "Or which of my creditors is it to whom I have sold you?"

151. Isaiah 50:2 – "Why, when I came, was there no man; why, when I called, was there no one to answer?"

152. Isaiah 50:2 – "Is my hand shortened that I cannot redeem?"

153. Isaiah 50:2 – "Or have I no power to deliver?"

154. Isaiah 51:12-13 – "I, I am he who comforts you; who are you that you are afraid of man who dies, of the son of man who is made like grass, and have forgotten the LORD your maker; who stretched out heavens and laid the foundations of the earth, and you fear continually all the day because of the wrath of the oppressor, when he sets himself to destroy?"

155. Isaiah 51:13 – "And where is the wrath of the oppressor?"

156. Isaiah 52:5 – "Now therefore what have I here," declares the LORD, "seeing that my people are taken away for nothing?"

157. Isaiah 55:2 – "Why do you spend your money for that which is not bread, and you labor for that which does not satisfy?"

158. Isaiah 57:4 – "Whom are you mocking?"

159. Isaiah 57:4 – "Against whom do you open your mouth wide and stick our your tongue?"

160. Isaiah 57:4-5 – "Are you not children of transgression, the off-spring of deceit, you who burn with lust among the oaks, under every

green tree, who slaughter your children in the valleys, under the clefts of rocks?"

161. Isaiah 57:6 – "Shall I relent for these things?"

162. Isaiah 57:11 – "Whom did you dread and fear, so that you lied, and did not remember me, did not lay it to heart?"

163. Isaiah 57:11 – "Have I not held my peace, even for a long time, and you do not fear me?"

164. Isaiah 58:6 – "Is not this the fast that I choose: to loose the bonds of wickedness, to undo the straps of the yoke, to let the oppressed go free, and to break every yoke?"

165. Isaiah 58:7 – "Is it not to share your bread with the hungry and bring the homeless poor into your house; when you see the naked, to cover him, and not to hide yourself from your own flesh?"

166. Isaiah 66:1 – "Thus says the LORD: 'Heaven is my throne, and the earth is my footstool; what is the house that you would build for me, and what is the place of my rest?'"

167. Isaiah 66:8 – "Who has heard such a thing?"

168. Isaiah 66:8 – "Who has seen such things?"

169. Isaiah 66:8 – "Shall a land be born in one day?"

170. Isaiah 66:8 – "Shall a nation be brought forth in one moment?"

171. Isaiah 66:9 – "Shall I bring to the point of birth and not cause to bring forth?"

172. Isaiah 66:9 – "Shall I, who cause to bring forth, shut the womb?"

173. Jeremiah 1:11 – "And the word of the LORD came to me, saying, 'Jeremiah, what do you see?'"

174. Jeremiah 1:13 – "The word of the LORD came to me a second time saying, 'What do you see?"

175. Jeremiah 2:4 – "What wrong did your fathers find in me that they went far from me, and went after worthlessness, and became worthless?"

176. Jeremiah 2:11 – "Has a nation changed its gods, even thought they are no gods?"

177. Jeremiah 2:14 – "Is Israel a slave?"

178. Jeremiah 2:14 – "Is he a home born servant?"

179. Jeremiah 2:14 – "Why then has be become prey?"

180. Jeremiah 2:17 – "Have you not brought this on upon yourself by forsaking the LORD your God, when he led you in the way?"

181. Jeremiah 2:18 – "And now what do you gain by going to Egypt to drink the waters of the Nile?"

182. Jeremiah 2:18 – "Or what do you gain by going to Assyria tot drink the waters of the Euphrates?"

183. Jeremiah 2:21 – "Yet I planted you a choice vine, wholly of pure seed. How then have you turned degenerate and become a wild vine?"

184. Jeremiah 2:23 – "How can you say 'I am not unclean, I have not gone after Baals'?"

185. Jeremiah 2:24 – "Who can restrain her lust?"

186. Jeremiah 2:28 – "But where are your gods you made for yourself?"

187. Jeremiah 2:29 – "Why do you contend with me?"

188. Jeremiah 2:31 – "Have I been a wilderness to Israel, or a land of thick darkness?"

189. Jeremiah 2:31 – "Why then do my people say 'We are free, we will come no more to you?'"

190. Jeremiah 2:32 – "Can a virgin forget her ornaments, or a bride her attire?"

191. Jeremiah 3:1 – "If a man divorces his wife and she goes from him and becomes another mans wife, will he return to her?"

192. Jeremiah 3:1 – "Would not that land be greatly polluted?"

193. Jeremiah 3:1 – "You have played the whore with many lovers; and would you return to me?"

194. Jeremiah 3:2 – "Where have you not been ravished?"

195. Jeremiah 3:6 – "Have you seen what she did, that faithless one, Israel, how she went up on every high hill and under every green tree, and there played the whore?"

196. Jeremiah 5:7 – "How can I pardon you?"

197. Jeremiah 5:9 – "Shall I not punish them for these things?"

198. Jeremiah 5:9 – "...and shall I not avenge my self on a nation such as this?"

199. Jeremiah 5:22 – "Do you not fear me?"

200. Jeremiah 5:22 – "Do you not tremble before me?"

201. Jeremiah 5:29 – "Shall I not punish them for these things?"

202. Jeremiah 5:29 – "...and shall I not avenge myself on a nation such as this?"

203. Jeremiah 6:15 – "Were they ashamed when they committed abomination?"

204. Jeremiah 6:20 – "What use to me is frankincense that comes from Sheba, or sweet cane from a distant land?"

205. Jeremiah 7:9 – "Will you steal, murder, commit adultery, swear falsely, make offerings to Baal, and go after other gods that you have not known, and then come and stand in this house, which is called by my name, and say 'We are delivered!' - only to go on doing all these abominations?"

206. Jeremiah 7:11 – "Has this house, which is called by my name, become a den of robbers in your eyes?"

207. Jeremiah 7:19 – "Is it I whom they provoke?"

208. Jeremiah 7:19 – "Is it not themselves to their own shame?"

209. Jeremiah 8:4 – "When men fall, do they not rise again?"

210. Jeremiah 8:4 – "If one turns away, does he not return?"

211. Jeremiah 8:5 – "Why then has this people turned away in perpetual backsliding?"

212. Jeremiah 8:8 – "How can you say 'We are wise, and the law of the LORD is with us'?"

213. Jeremiah 8:9 – "...behold they have rejected the word of the LORD, so what wisdom is in them?"

214. Jeremiah 8:12 – "Were they ashamed when they committed abomination?"

215. Jeremiah 9:7 – "Behold I will refine them and test them, for what else can I do because of my people?"

216. Jeremiah 9:9 – "Shall I not punish them for these things?"

217. Jeremiah 9:10 – "Shall I not avenge myself on a nation such as this?"

218. Jeremiah 11:15 – "What right has my beloved in my house, when she has done many vile deeds?"

219. Jeremiah 11:15 – "Can even sacrificial death avert your doom?"

220. Jeremiah 11:15 – "Can you then exult?"

221. Jeremiah 12:5 – "If you have raced with men on foot, and they have wearied you, how will you compete with horses?"

222. Jeremiah 12:5 – "And if in a safe land you are so trusting, what will you do in the thicket of the Jordan?"

223. Jeremiah 12:9 – "Is my heritage to me like a hyena's lair?"

224. Jeremiah 12:9 – "Are the birds of prey against her all around?"

225. Jeremiah 13:20 – "Where is the flock that was given you, your beautiful flock?"

226. Jeremiah 13:21 – "What will you say when they set as head over you those whom you yourself have taught to be friends to you?"

227. Jeremiah 13:21 – "Will not pangs take hold of you like those of a woman in labor?"

228. Jeremiah 15:5 – "Who will have pity on you, O Jerusalem, or who will grieve for you?"

229. Jeremiah 15:5 – "Who will turn aside to as about your welfare?"

230. Jeremiah 15:11 – "Have I not set you free for their good?"

231. Jeremiah 15:11 – "Have I not pleaded for you before the enemy in the time of trouble and in the time of distress?"

232. Jeremiah 15:12 – "Can one break iron, iron from the north, and bronze?"

233. Jeremiah 18:6 – "O house of Israel, can I not do with you as this potter has done?"

234. Jeremiah 18:13 – "Ask among the nations, Who has heard the like of this?"

235. Jeremiah 18:14 – "Does the snow of Lebanon leave the crags of Sirion?"

236. Jeremiah 18:14 – "Do the mountain waters run dry, the cold flowing streams?"

237. Jeremiah 22:15 – "Do you think you are a king because you compete in cedar?"

238. Jeremiah 22:15 – "Did not your father eat and drink and do justice and righteousness?"

239. Jeremiah 22:16 – "He judged the cause of the poor and needy; then it was well. Is not this to know me?"

240. Jeremiah 23:23 – "Am I a God at hand, declares the LORD, and not a God far away?"

241. Jeremiah 23:24 – "Can a man hide himself in secret places so that I cannot see him?"

242. Jeremiah 23:24 – "Do I not fill heaven and earth?"

243. Jeremiah 23:26 – "How long shall there be lies in the heart of the prophets who prophesy lies, and who prophesy the deceit of their own

heart, who think to make my people forget my name by their dreams that they tell one another, even as their fathers forgot my name for Baal?"

244. Jeremiah 23:28 – "What has straw in common with wheat?"

245. Jeremiah 23:29 – "Is not my word like fire, declares the LORD, and like a hammer that breaks the rock in pieces?"

246. Jeremiah 24:3 – "And the LORD said to me, "What do you see, Jeremiah?"

247. Jeremiah 25:29 – "For behold, I begin to work disaster at the city that is called by my name, and shall you go unpunished?"

248. Jeremiah 27:17 – "Why should this city become a desolation?"

249. Jeremiah 30:6 – "Ask now, and see, can a man bear a child?"

250. Jeremiah 30:6 – "Why then do I see every man with his hands on his stomach like a woman in labor?"

251. Jeremiah 30:6 – "Why has every face turned pale?"

252. Jeremiah 30:15 – "Why do you cry out over your hurt?"

253. Jeremiah 30:21 – "I will make him draw near, and he shall approach me, for who would dare of himself to approach me?" declares the LORD.

254. Jeremiah 31:20 – "Is Ephraim my dear son?"

255. Jeremiah 31:20 – "Is he my darling child?"

256. Jeremiah 31:22 – "How long will you waver, O faithless daughter?"

257. Jeremiah 32:27 – "Behold, I am the LORD, the God of all flesh. I anything too hard for me?"

258. Jeremiah 33:24 – "Have you not observed these people are saying 'The LORD has rejected the two clans that he chose'?"

259. Jeremiah 35:13 – "Thus says the LORD of hosts, the God of Israel: Go and say to the people of Judah and the inhabitants of Jerusalem, Will you not receive instruction and listen to my word?'"

260. Jeremiah 44:7 – "Why do you commit this great evil against yourselves, to cut off from you man and woman, infant and child, from the midst of Judah, leaving you no remnant?"

261. Jeremiah 44:8 – "Why do you provoke me to anger with thee works of your hands, making offerings to other gods in the land of Egypt where you have come to live, so that you may be cut off and become a curse and a taunt among all the nations of the earth?"

262. Jeremiah 44:9 – "Have you forgotten the evil of your fathers, the evil of the kings of Judah, the evil of their wives, your own evil, and the evil of your wives, which they committed in the land of Judah and in the streets of Jerusalem?"

263. Jeremiah 45:5 – "And do you seek great things for yourself?"

264. Jeremiah 46:5 – "Why have I seen it?"

265. Jeremiah 46:7 – "Who is this, rising like the Nile, like rivers whose waters surge?"

266. Jeremiah 48:14 – "How do you say 'We are heroes and mighty men of war'?"

267. Jeremiah 49:1 – "Has Israel no sons?"

268. Jeremiah 49:1 – "Has he no heir?"

269. Jeremiah 49:1 – "Why then has Milcom dispossed Gad, and his people settled in its cities?"

270. Jeremiah 49:4 – "Why do you boast of your valleys, O faithless daughter, who trusted in her treasures, saying, 'Who will come against me?'"

271. Jeremiah 49:7 – "Is wisdom no more in Teman?"

272. Jeremiah 49:7 – "Has counsel perished from the prudent?"

273. Jeremiah 49:7 – "Has their wisdom vanished?"

274. Jeremiah 49:9 – "If grape gatherers came to you, would they not leave gleanings?"

275. Jeremiah 49:9 – "If thieves came by night, would they not destroy only enough for themselves?"

276. Jeremiah 49:12 – "If those who did not deserve to drink the cup must drink it, will you go unpunished?"

277. Jeremiah 49:19 – "For who is like me?"

278. Jeremiah 49:19 – "Who will summon me?"

279. Jeremiah 49:19 – "What shepherd can stand before me?"

280. Jeremiah 49:25 – "How is the famous city not forsaken, the city of my joy?"

281. Jeremiah 50:44 – "For who is like me?"

282. Jeremiah 50:44 – "Who will summon me?"

283. Jeremiah 50:44 – "What shepherd can stand before me?"

284. Ezekiel 8:6 – "And he said to me, "Son of man, do you see what they are doing, the great abominations that the house of Israel are committing here, to drive me far from my sanctuary?"

285. Ezekiel 8:12 – "Then he said to me, "Son of man, have you seen what the elders of the house of Israel are doing in the dark, each in his room of pictures?"

286. Ezekiel 8:17 – "Then he said to me, 'Have you seen this, O son of man?"

287. Ezekiel 8:17 – "Is it too light a thing for the house of Judah to commit the abominations that they commit here, that they should fill the land with violence and provoke me still further to anger?"

288. Ezekiel 12:22 – "Son of man, what is this proverb that you have about the land of Israel, saying ;The days grow long, and every vision comes to nothing.'?"

289. Ezekiel 13:7 – "Have you not seen a false vision and uttered a lying divination, whenever you have said 'Declared the LORD', although I have not spoken?"

290. Ezekiel 13:12 – "And when the wall falls, will it not be said unto you, 'Where is the coating with which you smeared it?'"

291. Ezekiel 13:18 – "Will you hunt down souls belonging to my people and keep your own souls alive?"

292. Ezekiel 14:3 – "Should I let myself be consulted by them?"

293. Ezekiel 15:2 – "Son of man, how does the wood of the vine surpass any wood, the vine branch that is among the trees of the forest?"

294. Ezekiel 15:3 – "Is wood taken from it to make anything?"

295. Ezekiel 15:3 – "Do people take a peg from it to hang any vessel on it?"

296. Ezekiel 15:4 – "Behold it is given to the fire for fuel. When the first has consumed both ends of it, and the middle of it is charred, is it useful for anything?"

297. Ezekiel 16:43 – "Have you not committed lewdness in addition to all your abominations?"

298. Ezekiel 16:56 – "Was not your sister Sodom a byword in your mouth in the day of your pride, before your wickedness was uncovered?"

299. Ezekiel 17:9 – "Say, Thus says the LORD God: Will it thrive?"

300. Ezekiel 17:9 – "Will he not pull up its roots and cut off its fruit, so that it withers, so that all its fresh sprouting leaves wither?"

301. Ezekiel 17:10 – "Behold, it is planted: will it thrive?"

302. Ezekiel 17:10 – "Will it not utterly wither when the east wind strikes it - wither away on the bed where it sprouted?"

303. Ezekiel 17:12 – "Do you not know what these things mean?"

304. Ezekiel 17:15 – "Will he thrive?"

305. Ezekiel 17:15 – "Can one escape who does such things?"

306. Ezekiel 17:15 – "Can he break the covenant and yet escape?"

307. Ezekiel 18:2 – "What do you mean by repeating this proverb concerning the land of Israel, 'The fathers have eaten sour grapes, and the children's teeth are set on edge.'?"

308. Ezekiel 18:13 – "...lends at interest, and takes profit; shall he then live?"

309. Ezekiel 18:23 – "Have I any pleasure in the death of the wicked, declares the LORD God, and not rather that he should turn from his way and live?"

310. Ezekiel 18:24 – "But when a righteous person turns away from his righteousness and does injustice and does the same abominations that the wicked person does, shall he live?"

311. Ezekiel 18:25 – "Hear now, O house of Israel: Is my way not just?"

312. Ezekiel 18:25 – "Is it not your ways that are not just?"

313. Ezekiel 18:29 – "O house of Israel, are my ways not just?"

314. Ezekiel 18:20 – "Is it not your ways that are not just?"

315. Ezekiel 18:31 – "Cast away from you all the transgressions that you have committed, and make yourselves a new heart and a new spirit! Why will you die, O house of Israel?"

316. Ezekiel 20:3 – "Is it to inquire of me that you come?"

317. Ezekiel 20:4 – "Will you judge them, son of man, will you judge them?"

318. Ezekiel 20:29 – "I said to them, 'What is the high place to which you go?'"

319. Ezekiel 20:30 – "Will you defile yourselves after the manner of your fathers and go whoring after their detestable things?"

320. Ezekiel 20:31 – "When you present you or gifts and offer up your children in fire, you defile yourselves with all your idols to this day. And shall I be inquired of by you, O house of Israel?"

321. Ezekiel 21:13 – "For it will not be a testing – what could it do if you despise the rod? declares the LORD."

322. Ezekiel 22:14 – "Can your courage endure, or can your hands be strong, in the days that I shall deal with you?"

323. Ezekiel 23:36 – "The LORD said to me: 'Son of man, will you judge Oholah and Oholibah?"

324. Ezekiel 26:15 – "Thus says the LORD God to Tyre: Will non the coastlands shake at the sound of your fall, when the wounded groan, when slaughter is made in your midst?"

325. Ezekiel 28:9 – "Will you still say 'I am a god' , in the presence of those who kill you, though you are but a man, and no god, in the hands of those who slay you?"

326. Ezekiel 31:2 – "Who are you in your greatness?"

327. Ezekiel 31:18 – "Whom are you thus like in glory and in greatness among the trees of Eden?"

328. Ezekiel 32:19 – "Whom do you surpass in beauty?"

329. Ezekiel 33:11 – "Say to them, As I live, declares the LORD God, I have no pleasure in the death of the wicked, but that the wicked turn from his way and live; turn back, turn back from your evil ways, for why will you die, O House of Israel?"

330. Ezekiel 33:25 – "Therefore say to them, 'Thus says the LORD God: You eat flesh with the blood and lift up your eyes to your idols and shed blood; shall you then possess the land?"

331. Ezekiel 33:26 – "You rely on the sword, you commit abominations, and each of you defiles his neighbor's wife; shall you then possess the land?"

332. Ezekiel 34:2 – "Thus says the LORD God: Ah, shepherds of Israel who have been feeding yourselves! Should not shepherds feed the sheep?"

333. Ezekiel 34:18 – "Is it not enough for you to feed on the good pasture, that you must tread down with your feet the rest of your pasture, and to drink of clear water, that you must muddy the rest of the water with your feet?"

334. Ezekiel 34:19 – "And must my sheep eat what you have trodden with your feet, and drink what you have muddied with your feet?"

335. Ezekiel 37:3 – "And he said to me, 'Son of man, can these bones live?"

336. Ezekiel 38:14 – "Thus says the LORD God: On that day when my people Israel are dwelling securely will you no know it?"

337. Ezekiel 38:17 – "Thus says the LORD God: Are you he of whom I spoke in former days by my servants through the prophets of Israel, who in those days prophesied for years that I would bring you against them?"

338. Ezekiel 47:8 – "And he said to me, 'Son of man have you seen this?"

339. Hosea 6:4 – "What shall I do with you, O Ephraim?"

340. Hosea 6:4 – "What shall I do with you, O Judah?"

341. Hosea 8:5 – "How long will they be incapable of innocence?"

342. Hosea 10:9 – "Shall not the war against the unjust overtake them in Gibeah?"

343. Hosea 11:8 – "How can I give you up, O Ephraim?"

344. Hosea 11:8 – "How can I hand you over, O Israel?"

345. Hosea 11:8 – "How can I make you like Admah?"

346. Hosea 11:8 – "How can I treat you like Zebolim?"

347. Hosea 13:10 – "Where not is your king, to save you in all your cities?"

348. Hosea 13:10 – "Where are all your rulers - those of whom you said 'Give me a king and princes?'"

349. Hosea 13:14 – "O Death, where are your plagues?"

350. Hosea 13:14 – "O Sheol, where is your sting?"

351. Hosea 14:8 – "O Ephraim, what have I to do with idols?"

352. Joel 1:2 – "Has such a thing happened in your days, or in the days of your fathers?"

353. Joel 3:4 – "What are you to me, O Tyre and Sidon, and all the regions of Philistia?"

354. Joel 3:4 – "Are you paying me back for something?"

355. Amos 2:11 – "And I raised up some of your sons for prophets, and some of your young men for Nazirites. Is it not indeed so, O people of Israel?' declares the LORD."

356. Amos 3:3 – "Do two walk together, unless they have agreed to meet?"

357. Amos 3:4 – "Does a lion roar in the forest when he has no prey?"

358. Amos 3:4 – "Does a young lion cry out from his den, if he has taken nothing?"

359. Amos 3:5 – "Does a bird fall in a snare on the earth, when there is no trap for it?"

360. Amos 3:5 – "Does a snare spring up from the ground, when it has taken nothing?"

361. Amos 3:6 – "Is a trumpet blown in a city, and the people are not afraid?"

362. Amos 3:6 – "Does disaster come to a city unless the LORD has done it?"

363. Amos 3:8 – "The lion has roared; who will not fear?"

364. Amos 3:8 – "The LORD has spoken; who can but prophesy?"

365. Amos 5:25 – "Did you bring to me sacrifices and offerings during the forty years in the wilderness, O house of Israel?"

366. Amos 6:2 – "Are you better than these kingdoms?"

367. Amos 6:3 – "Or is their territory greater than your territory, O you who put far away the day of disaster and bring near the seat of violence?"

368. Amos 7:8 – "And the LORD said to me, "Amos, what do you see?"

369. Amos 8:2 – "And the LORD said to me, "Amos, what do you see?"

370. Amos 8:8 – "Shall not the land tremble on this account, and everyone mourn who dwells in it, and all of it rise like the Nile, and be tossed about and sink again, like the Nile of Egypt?"

371. Amos 9:7 – "Are you not like the Cushites to me, O people of Israel?' declares the LORD."

372. Amos 9:7 – "Did I not bring up Israel from the land of Egypt, and the Philistines from Caphtor and the Syrians from Kir?"

373. Obadiah 1:5 – "If thieves came to you, if plunderers came by night - how you have been destroyed! - would they not steal only enough for themselves?"

374. Obadiah 1:5 – "If grape gatherers came to you, would they not leave gleanings?"

375. Obadiah 1:8 – "Will I not on that day, declares the LORD, destroy the wise men out of Edom, and understanding out of Mount Esau?"

376. Jonah 4:4 – "Do you do well to be angry?"

377. Jonah 4:9 – "Do you do well to be angry for the plant?"

378. Jonah 4:11 – "And should I not pity Nineveh, that great city, in which there are more than 120,000 persons who do not know their right hand from their left, and also much cattle?"

379. Micah 6:3 – "O my people, what have I done to you?"

380. Micah 6:3 – "How have I wearied you?"

381. Micah 6:10 – "Can I forget any longer the treasures of wickedness in the house of the wicked, and the scant measure that is accursed?"

382. Micah 6:11 – "Shall I acquit the man with wicked scales and with a bag of deceitful weights?"

383. Nahum 3:7 – "Where shall I seek comforters for you?"

384. Nahum 3:8 – "Are you better than Thebes that sat by the Nile, with water around her, her rampart a sea and water her wall?"

385. Nahum 3:19 – "For upon whom has not come your unceasing evil?"

386. Haggai 1:4 – "Is it a time for you yourselves to dwell in your paneled houses, while this house lies in ruins?"

387. Haggai 1:9 – "You looked for much, and behold, it came to little. And when you brought it home, I blew it away. Why?"

388. Haggai 2:3 – "Who is left among you who saw this house in its former glory?"

389. Haggai 2:3 – "How do you see it now?"

390. Haggai 2:3 – "Is it not as nothing in your eyes?"

391. Haggai 2:11-12 – "Thus says the LORD of hosts: Ask the priests about the law: 'If someone carries holy meat in the fold of his garment and touches with his fold bread or stew or wine or oil or any kind of food, does it become holy?"

392. Haggai 2:15-16 – "Before stone was placed upon stone in the temple of the LORD, how did you fare?"

393. Haggai 2:19 – "Is the seed yet in the barn?"

394. Zechariah 1:5 – "Your fathers, where are they?"

395. Zechariah 1:5 – "And the prophets, do they live forever?"

396. Zechariah 1:6 – "But my words and my statutes, which I commanded my servants the prophets, did they not overtake your fathers?"

397. Zechariah 7:5 – "Say to all the people of the land and the priests, 'When you fasted and mourned in the fifth month and in the seventh, for these seventy years, was it for me that you fasted?"

398. Zechariah 7:6 – "And when you eat and when you drink, do you not ear for yourselves and drink for yourselves?"

399. Zechariah 7:7 – "Were not these the words that the LORD proclaimed by the former prophets, when Jerusalem was inhabited and prosperous, with her cities around her, and the South and the lowland were inhabited?"

400. Zechariah 8:6 – "Thus says the LORD of hosts: If it is marvelous in the sight of the remnant of this people in those days, should it also be marvelous in my sight, declares the LORD of hosts?"

401. Malachi 1:2 – "Is not Esau Jacob's brother?"

402. Malachi 1:6 – "If then I am a father, where is my honor?"

403. Malachi 1:6 – "And if I am a master, where is my fear?"

404. Malachi 1:8 – "When you offer blind animals in sacrifice, is that not evil?"

405. Malachi 1:8 – "And when you offer those that are lame or sick, is that not evil?"

406. Malachi 1:8 – "Present that to your governor; will he accept you or show you favor?"

407. Malachi 1:9 – "With such a gift from your hand, will he show favor to any of you?"

408. Malachi 1:13 – "Shall I accept that from your hand?"

409. Malachi 3:2 – "But who can endure the day of his coming, ad who can stand when he appears?"

410. Malachi 3:8 – "Will a man rob God?"

411. Matthew 5:13 – "You are the salt of the earth, but if the salt has lost its taste, how shall its saltiness be restored?"

412. Matthew 5:46 – "For if you love those that love you, what reward do you have?"

413. Matthew 5:46 – "Do not even the tax collectors do the same?"

414. Matthew 5:47 – "And if you greet only your own brothers, what more are you doing than others?"

415. Matthew 5:47 – "Do not even the gentiles do the same?"

416. Matthew 6:25 – "Is not life more than food, and the body more than clothing?"

417. Matthew 6:26 – "Are you not of more value than they?"

418. Matthew 6:27 – "And which of you by being anxious can add a single hour to his span of life?"

419. Matthew 6:28 – "And why are you anxious about clothing?"

420. Matthew 6:30 – "But if God so clothes the grass of the field, which today is alive and tomorrow is thrown into the oven, will he not much more clothe you, O you of little faith?"

421. Matthew 7:3 – "Why do you see the speck that is in your brother's eye, but do not notice the log that is in your own eye?"

422. Matthew 7:4 – "Or how can you say to your brother, 'let me take the spec out of your eye' when there is the log in your own eye?"

423. Matthew 7:9 – "Or which one of you, if his son asks him for bread, will give him a stone?"

424. Matthew 7:10 – "Or if he asks for a fish, will give him a serpent?"

425. Matthew 7:16 – "You will recognize them by their fruits. Are grapes gathered from thornbushes, or figs from thistles?"

426. Matthew 8:26 – "Why are you afraid, O you of little faith?"

427. Matthew 9:4 – "But Jesus, knowing their thoughts said, 'Why do you think evil in your hearts?'"

428. Matthew 9:5 – "For which is easier to say, 'Your sins are forgiven' or to say 'rise and walk'?"

429. Matthew 9:15 – "And Jesus said to them 'Can the wedding guests mourn as long as the bridegroom is with them?'"

430. Matthew 9:28 – "When he entered the house, the blind men came to him, and Jesus said to them 'Do you believe that I am able to do this?"

431. Matthew 10:29 – "Are not two sparrows sold for a penny?"

432. Matthew 11:7 – "As they went away, Jesus began to speak to the crowds concerning John: 'What did you go out into the wilderness to see?"

433. Matthew 11:7 – "A reed shaken by the wind?"

434. Matthew 11:8 – "What then did you go out to see?"

435. Matthew 11:8 – "A man dressed in soft clothing?"

436. Matthew 11:9 – "Then what did you go out to see?"

437. Matthew 11:9 – "A prophet?"

438. Matthew 11:16 – "But to what shall I compare this generation?"

439. Matthew 11:23 – "And you, Capernaum, will you be exalted to heaven?"

440. Matthew 12:3 – "Have you not read what David did when he was hungry, and those who were with him: how he entered the house of God and ate the bread of the Presence, which it was not lawful for him to eat nor for those who were with him but only the priests?"

441. Matthew12:5 – "Or have you not read in the law how on the Sabbath the priests in the temple profane the Sabbath and are guiltless?"

442. Matthew 12:11 – "Which one of you who has a sheep, if it falls into a pit on the Sabbath, will not take hold of it and lift it out?"

443. Matthew 12:26 – "And if Satan casts out Satan, he is divided against himself. How then will his kingdom stand?"

444. Matthew 12:27 – "And if I cast out demons by Beelzebul, by whom do your sons cast them out?"

445. Matthew 12:29 – "Or how can someone enter a strongman's house and plunder his goods, unless he first binds the strong man?"

446. Matthew 12:34 – "You brood of vipers! How can you speak good, when you are evil?"

447. Matthew 12:48 – "But he replied to the man who told him, 'Who is my mother, and who are my brothers?"

448. Matthew 13:51 – "Have you understood all these things?"

449. Matthew 14:31 – "Jesus immediately reached out his hand and took hold of him, saying to him, 'O you of little faith, why did you doubt?"

450. Matthew 15:3 – "And why do you break the commandment of God for the sake of your tradition?"

451. Matthew 15:16 – "And he said, 'Are you also still without understanding?"

452. Matthew 15:17 – "Do you not see that whatever goes into the mouth passes into the stomach and is expelled?"

453. Matthew 15:34 – "And Jesus said to them, 'How many loaves do you have?"

454. Matthew 16:8 – "But Jesus, aware of this, said, 'O you of little faith, why are you discussing among yourselves that fact that you have no bread?"

455. Matthew 16:9 – "Do you not yet perceive?"

456. Matthew 16:9 – "Do you not remember the five loaves for the five thousand, and how many baskets you gathered?"

457. Matthew 16:10 – "Or the seven loaves for the four thousand, and how many baskets you gathered?"

458. Matthew 16:11 – "How is it that you fail to understand that I did no speak about bread?"

459. Matthew 16:13 – "Now when Jesus came into the district of Caesarea Philippi, he asked his disciples, "Who do people say that the Son of Man is?"

460. Matthew 16:15 – "But who do you say that I am?"

461. Matthew 16:26 – "For what will it profit a man if he gains the whole world and forfeits his soul?"

462. Matthew 16:26 – "Or what shall a man give in return for his soul?"

463. Matthew 17:17 – "And Jesus answered, 'O faithless and twisted generation, how long am I to be with you?"

464. Matthew 17:17 – "How long am I to bear with you?"

465. Matthew 17:25 – "And when he came into the house, Jesus spoke to him first, saying 'What do you think Simon?"

466. Matthew 17:25 – "From whom do kings of the earth take toll or tax?"

467. Matthew 17:25 – "From their sons or others?"

468. Matthew 18:12 – "What do you think?"

469. Matthew 18:12 – "If a man has a hundred sheep, and one of them has gone astray, does he not leave the ninety-nine on the mountains and go in search of the one that went astray?"

470. Matthew 19:4 – "He answered, 'Have you not read that he who created them from the beginning made them male and female and said 'Therefore a man shall leave his father and his mother and hold fast to his wife, and the two shall become one flesh?'"

471. Matthew 19:17 – "And he said to him, 'Why do you ask me about what is good?"

472. Matthew 20:21 – "And he said to her, 'What do you want?'"

473. Matthew 20:22 – "Jesus answered, 'You do not know what you are asking. Are you able to drink the cup that I am to drink?"

474. Matthew 20:32 – "And stopping, Jesus called them and said, 'What do you want me to do for you?'"

475. Matthew 21:25 – "The baptism of John, from where did it come?"

476. Matthew 21:25 – "From heaven or from man?"

477. Matthew 21:28 – "What do you think?"

478. Matthew 21:31 – "Which of the two did the will of his father?"

479. Matthew 21:40 – "When therefore the owner of the vineyard comes, what will he do to those tenants?"

480. Matthew 21:42 – "Jesus said to them, 'Have you never read in the Scriptures: 'The stone that the builders rejected has become the cornerstone; this was the Lord's doing, and it is marvelous in our eyes'?'"

481. Matthew 22:18 – "But Jesus, aware of their malice, said, 'Why put me to the test, you hypocrites?"

482. Matthew 22:20 – "And Jesus said to them, "Whose likeness and inscription is this?"

483. Matthew 22:31 – "And as for the resurrection of the dead, have you not read what was said to you by God: 'I am the God of Abraham, and the God of Isaac, and the God of Jacob'? He is not the God of the dead, but of the living."

484. Matthew 22:41-42 – "Now while the Pharisees were gathered together, Jesus asked them a question, saying 'What do you think about the Christ?'"

485. Matthew 22:42 – "Whose son is he?"

486. Matthew 22:43 – "He said to them 'How is it them that David, in the Spirit, call him Lord, saying 'The Lord said to my Lord, sit at my right hand, until I put your enemies under your feet?'"

487. Matthew 22:45 – "If then David calls him Lord, how is he his son?"

488. Matthew 23:17 – "You blind fools! For which is greater, the gold or the temple that has made the gold sacred?"

489. Matthew 23:19 – "You blind men! For which is greater, the gift or the altar that makes the gift sacred?"

490. Matthew 23:33 – "You serpents, you brood of vipers, how are you to escape being sentenced to hell?"

491. Matthew 24:2 – "You see all these, do you not?"

492. Matthew 24:45 – "Who then is he faithful and wise servant, whom his master has set over his household, to give them their food at the proper time?"

493. Matthew 26:10 – "But Jesus, aware of this, said to them, 'Why do yo trouble this woman?"

494. Matthew 26:40 – "And he came to the disciples and found them sleeping. And he said to Peter, 'So, could you not watch with me one hour?'"

495. Matthew 26:53 – "Do you think that I cannot appeal to my Father, and he will at once send me more than twelve legions of angels?"

496. Matthew 26:54 – "But how then should the Scriptures be fulfilled, that it must be so?"

497. Matthew 26:55 – "At that time Jesus said to the crowds, 'Have you come out as against a robber, with swords and clubs to capture me?"

498. Matthew 27:46 – "And about the ninth hour Jesus cried out with a loud voice, saying "Eli, Eli, lema sabachthani?" that is "my God, my God, why have you forsaken me?"

499. Mark 3:4 – "And he said to them, 'Is it lawful on the Sabbath to do good or to do harm, to save life or to kill?"

500. Mark 4:13 – "And he said to them, 'Do you not understand this parable?'"

501. Mark 4:13 – "How then will you understand all the parables?"

502. Mark 4:21 – "And he said to them, 'Is a lamp brought in to be put under a basket, or under a bed, and not on a stand?"

503. Mark 4:30 – "And he said, 'With what can we compare the kingdom of God, or what parable shall we use for it?'

504. Mark 5:9 – "And Jesus asked him, 'What is your name?'"

505. Mark 5:30 – "And Jesus, having perceiving in himself that power had gone out from him, immediately turned about in the crowd and said 'Who touched my garments?'"

506. Mark 5:39 –"And when he had entered, he said to them, 'Why are you making a commotion and weeping?"

507. Mark 8:12 – "And he sighed deeply in his spirit and said, 'Why does this generation seek a sign?'"

508. Mark 8:23 – "And he took the blind man by the hand and led him out of the village, and when he had spit on his eyes and laid his hands on him, he asked him 'Do you see anything'?"

509. Mark 8:16 – "And he asked them, 'What are you arguing about with them?'"

510. Mark 10:3 – "He answered them, 'What did Moses command you?'"

511. Mark 11:17 – "And he was teaching them and saying to them, 'Is it not written, 'May house shall be called a house of prayer for all nations'? But you have made it a den of robbers.'"

512. Mark 12:24 – "Jesus said to them, 'Is this not the reason you are wrong, because you know neither the Scriptures not the power of God?'"

513. Mark 12:41 – "And he came the third time and said to them, 'Are you still sleeping and taking your rest?'"

514. Mark 12:48 – "And Jesus said to them, 'Have you come out as against a robber, with swords and clubs to capture me?'"

515. Luke 3:49 – "And he said to them, 'Why were you looking for me?'"

516. Luke 3:49 – "Did you not know that I must be in my father's house?"

517. Luke 6:34 – "And if you lend to those from whom you expect to receive, what credit is that to you?"

518. Luke 6:39 – "Can a blind man lead a blind man?"

519. Luke 6:39 – "Will they not both fall into a pit?"

520. Luke 6:46 – "Why do you call me 'Lord, Lord', and not do what I tell you?"

521. Luke 7:42 – "Now which of them will love him more?"

522. Luke 8:30 – "Jesus then asked him, 'What is your name?'"

523. Luke 10:26 – "What is written in the law?"

524. Luke 10:26 – "How do you read it?"

525. Luke 10:36 – "Which of these three, do you think, proved to be a neighbor to the man who fell among the robbers?"

526. Luke 11:5 – "Which of you who has a friend will go to him at midnight and say to him, 'Friend, lend me three loaves, for a friend of mine has arrived on a journey, and I have nothing to set before him'; and he will answer from within, 'Do not bother me; the door is now shut, and my children are with me in bed. I cannot get up and give you anything.'?"

527. Luke 11:11 – "What father among you, if his son asks for a fish, will instead of a fish give him a serpent?"

528. Luke 11:12 – "...or if he asks for an egg, will give him a scorpion?"

529. Luke 11:40 – "You fools! Did not he who made the outside make the inside also?"

530. Luke 12:14 – "Man who made me a judge or arbitrator over you?"

531. Luke 12:20 – "But God said to him, 'Fool! This night your soul is required of you, and the things you have prepared, whose will they be?"

532. Luke 12:26 – "If then you are not able to do as small a thing as that, why are you anxious about the rest?"

533. Luke 12:42 – "And the Lord said, 'Who then is the faithful and wise manager, whom his master will set over his household, to give them their portion of food at the proper time?'"

534. Luke 12:31 – "Do you think that I have come to give peace on earth?"

535. Luke 12:57 – "And why do you not judge for yourselves what is right?"

536. Luke 13:2 – "And he answered them, 'Do you think that these Galileans were worse sinners than all the other Galileans, because they suffered in this way?'"

537. Luke 13:4 – "Or those eighteen on whom the tower in Siloam fell and killed them; do you think that they were worse offenders than all the others who lived in Jerusalem?"

538. Luke 13:15 – "You hypocrites! Does not each of you on the Sabbath untie his ox or his donkey from the manger and lead it away to water it?"

539. Luke 13:16 – "And ought not this daughter of Abraham whom Satan bound for eighteen years, be loosed from this bond on the Sabbath day?"

540. Luke 13:18 – "He said therefore, 'What is the kingdom of God like?"

541. Luke 13:18 – "And to what shall I compare it?"

542. Luke 13:20 – "And again he said, 'To what shall I compare the Kingdom of God?'"

543. Luke 14:28 – "For which of you, desiring to build a tower, does not first sit down and count the cost, whether he has enough to complete it?"

544. Luke 14:31 – "Or what king, going out to encounter another king in war, will not sit down first and deliberate whether he is able with ten thousand to meet him who comes against him with twenty thousand?"

545. Luke 15:8 – "Or what woman, having ten silver coins, if she loses on coin, does not light a lamp and sweep the house and seek diligently until she finds it?"

546. Luke 16:11 – "If then you have not been faithful in the unrighteous wealth, who will entrust to you true riches?"

547. Luke 16:12 – "And if you have not been faithful in that which is another's, who will give you that which is your own?"

548. Luke 17:7 – "Will any one of you who has a servant plowing or keeping sheep say to him when he has come in from the field, 'Come at once and recline at the table?"

549. Luke 17:8 – "Will he not rather say to him, 'Prepare supper for me, and dress properly, and serve me while I eat and drink, and afterward you will eat and drink'?"

550. Luke 17:9 – "Does he thank the servant because he did what was commanded?"

551. Luke 17:17 – "Then Jesus answered, 'Were not ten cleansed?'"

552. Luke 17:17 – "Where are the nine?"

553. Luke 17:18 – "Was no one found to return and give praise to God except this foreigner?"

554. Luke 18:7 – "And will not God give justice to his elect, who cry to him day and night?"

555. Luke 18:7 – "Will he delay long over them?"

556. Luke 18:8 – "I tell you, he will give justice to them speedily. Nevertheless, when the Son of Man comes, will he find faith on earth?"

557. Luke 18:41 – "What do you want me to do for you?"

558. Luke 22:27 – "For who is the greater, one who reclines at the table or one who serves?"

559. Luke 22:27 – "Is it not the one who reclines at the table?"

560. Luke 22:48 – "Judas would you betray the Son of Man with a kiss?"

561. Luke 23:31 – "For if they do these things when the wood is green, what will happen when it is dry?"

562. Luke 24:17 – "And he said to them, 'What is this conversation that you are holding with each other as you walk?'"

563. Luke 24:19 – "And he said to them, 'What things?'"

564. Luke 24:26 – "Was it not necessary that the Christ should suffer these things and enter into his glory?"

565. Luke 24:38 – "And he said to them, 'Why are you troubled, and why do doubts arise in your hearts?'"

566. Luke 24:41 – "Have you anything here to eat?"

567. John 1:38 – "Jesus turned and saw them following and said to them, 'What are you seeking?'"

568. John 1:50 – "Jesus answered him, 'Because I said to you 'I saw you under the fig tree' do you believe?'"

569. John 2:4 – "And Jesus said to her, 'Woman, what does that have to do with me?'"

570. John 3:10 – "Jesus answered him, 'Are you a teacher of Israel and yet you do not understand these things?'"

571. John 3:12 – "If I have told you earthly things and you do not believe, how can you believe if I tell you heavenly things?"

572. John 4:35 – "Do you not say, 'There are yet four months, then comes the harvest?'"

573. John 5:6 – "When Jesus saw him lying there and knew that he had already been there a long time, he said to him, 'Do you want to be healed?'"

574. John 5:44 – "How can you believe, when you receive glory from one another and do not seek the glory that comes from the only God?"

575. John 5:47 – "But if you do not believe his writings, how will you believe my words?"

576. John 6:5 – "Lifting up his eyes, then, and seeing that a large crowd was coming toward him, Jesus said to Philip, 'Where are we to buy bread, so that these people may eat?"

577. John 6:61 – "But Jesus, knowing in himself that his disciples were grumbling about this, said to them, 'Do you take offense at his?'"

578. John 6:62 – "Then what if you were to see the Son of Man ascending to where he was before?"

579. John 6:67 – "So Jesus said to the twelve, 'Do you want to go away as well?'"

580. John 6:60 – "Jesus answered them, 'Did I not choose you, the twelve?"

581. John 7:19 – "Has not Moses given you the law? Yet none of you keeps the law."

582. John 7:19 – "Why do you seek to kill me?"

583. John 7:23 – "If on the Sabbath a man receives circumcision, so that the law of Moses may not be broken, are you angry with me because on the Sabbath I made a man's whole body well?"

584. John 8:10 – "Jesus stood up and said to her, 'Woman, where are they?"

585. John 8:10 – "Has no one condemned you?"

586. John 8:43 – "Why do you not understand what I say?"

587. John 8:46 – "Which one of you convicts me of sin?"

588. John 8:46 – "If I tell the truth, why do you not believe me?"

589. John 9:35 – "Jesus heard that they had cast him out, and having found him he said, 'Do you believe in the Son of Man?'"

590. John 10:32 – "Jesus answered them, 'I have shown you many good works from the Father; for which of them are you going to stone me?'"

591. John 10:34 – "Jesus answered them, 'Is it not written in you Law, 'I said, you are gods'?'"

592. John 10:35 – "If he called them gods to whom the word of God came - and Scripture cannot be broken - do you say of him whom the Father consecrated and sent into the world, 'You are blaspheming,' because I said, 'I am the Son of God'?'"

593. John 11:9 – "Jesus answered, 'Are there not twelve hours in the day?"

594. John 11:26 – "...and everyone who lives and believes in me shall never die. Do you believe this?"

595. John 11:34 – "And he said, 'Where have you laid him?'"

596. John 11:40 – "Jesus said to her, 'Did I not tell you that if you believed you would see the glory of God?'"

597. John 12:27 – "Now is my soul troubled. And what shall I say - 'Father save me from this hour?'"

598. John 13:12 – When he had washed their feet and put on his outer garments and resumed his place, he said to them, 'Do you understand what I have done to you?"

599. John 13:38 – "Jesus answered, 'Will you lay down your life for me?"

600. John 14:2 – "In my Father's house are many rooms. If it were not so, would I have told you that I go to prepare a place for you?"

601. John 14:9 – "Jesus said to him, 'Have I been with you so long, and you still do not know me, Philip?"

602. John 14:9 – "Whoever has seen me, has seen the Father. Howe can you say 'Show us the Father?'"

603. John 14:10 – "Do you not believe that I am in the Father and the Father is in me?"

604. John 16:19 – "Jesus knew that they wanted to ask him, so he said to them, 'Is this what you are asking yourselves what I meant by saying, 'A little while and you will not see me, and again a little while and you will see me?'"

605. John 16:31 – "Do you know believe?"

606. John 18:4 – "Then Jesus, knowing all that would happen to him, came forward and said to them, 'Whom do you seek?'"

607. John 18:7 – "So he asked them again, 'Whom do you seek?'"

608. John 18:11 – "So Jesus said to Peter, 'Put your sword into its sheath; shall I not drink the cup that the Father has given me?"

609. John 18:21 – "Why do you ask me?"

610. John 18:23 – "Jesus answered him, 'If what I said is wrong, bear witness about the wrong; but if what I said is right, why do you strike me?"

611. John 18:34 – "Jesus answered, 'Do you say this of your own accord, or did others say it to you about me?'"

612. John 20:15 – "Jesus said to her, 'Woman, why are you weeping?"

613. John 20:15 – "Whom are you seeking?"

614. John 20:29 – "Jesus said to him, 'Have you believed because you have seen me?"

615. John 21:5 – "Jesus said to them, 'Children do you have any fish?'"

616. John 21:15 – "When they had finished breakfast, Jesus said to Simon Peter, 'Simon, son of John, do you love me more than these?'"

617. John 21:16 – "He said to him a second time, 'Simon, son of John, do you love me?'"

618. John 21:17 – "He said to him the third time, 'Do you love me?'"

619. John 21:22 – "Jesus said to him, 'If it is my will that he remain until I come, what is that to you? You follow me!"

620. Acts 9:4 – "And falling to the ground, he heard a voice saying to him, 'Saul, Saul, why are you persecuting me?'"